The
High
Achiever's
Guide to
HAPPINESS

VANCE CAESAR
CAROL ANN CAESAR

CORWIN PRESS
A SAGE Publications Company
Thousand Oaks, California

For information:

Corwin Press
A Sage Publications Company
2455 Teller Road
Thousand Oaks, California 91320
www.corwinpress.com

Sage Publications Ltd.
1 Oliver's Yard
55 City Road
London EC1Y 1SP
United Kingdom

Sage Publications India Pvt. Ltd.
B-42, Panchsheel Enclave
Post Box 4109
New Delhi 110 017 India

Printed in the United States of America

Library of Congress Cataloging-in-Publication Data

Caesar, Vance.
The high achiever's guide to happiness / Vance Caesar, Carol Ann Caesar.
    p. cm.
Includes bibliographical references.
ISBN 1-4129-1612-7 (cloth) — ISBN 1-4129-1613-5 (pbk.)
    1. Leadership. 2. Success. 3. Success in business. 4. Happiness.
5. Successful people. I. Caesar, Carol Ann. II. Title.
HD57.7.C34 2006
650.1—dc22

                                                              2005019389

This book is printed on acid-free paper.

05 06 07 08 09   10 9 8 7 6 5 4 3 2 1

Acquisitions Editor:	Elizabeth Brenkus
Editorial Assistant:	Candice L. Ling
Production Editor:	Melanie Birdsall
Copyeditor:	Bill Bowers, Interactive Composition Corporation
Typesetter:	C&M Digitals (P) Ltd.
Proofreader:	Teresa Herlinger
Cover Designer:	Michael Dubowe
Production Artist:	Anthony Paular

Contents

Dedication

This is our effort to condense research and our many experiences, both personal and professional, into a model that empowers high achievers and those on the road to high achieving to also experience their own happiness.

We believe that when achievers find their own happiness, they will pass along something very positive to others, creating a chain that spreads for the betterment of communities and the planet. A theme for this is that much is expected of those who have been given much.

The question we pose for you: Will you do your part to create your own true happiness and then, as a consequence, radiate that outward? To those of you who accept and work toward this goal, we dedicate this book.

Acknowledgments

Web both are grateful to all of the many teachers, coaches, and mentors we have had throughout our lives, personally and professionally. They have so richly shared their experiences, knowledge, wisdom, and caring. This has made our lives better and allowed us to build upon their work to evolve our beliefs about what creates happiness for high achievers.

We would not be able to do the work we do without the tremendous support we receive from so many. While it is not reasonable to list everyone, there are some whom we especially want to thank. The people who work with us on a daily basis are always asking what else they can do to help. We thank Brooke Bischoff, Colleen Romero, Linda Kau, Amanda Stahl, and Leslie Evans for all that they do and for who they are.

We are grateful to our clients, who have invited us into their lives. They have given us the opportunity to learn more and to be on the path with them. We thank them for our lives being more meaningful.

We thank our family for their understanding as we have spent time on this project.

We are grateful for the patience and latitude we are able to give to each other. This has allowed us to grow and evolve over the span of a 38-year marriage.

Corwin Press gratefully acknowledges the contributions of the following individuals:

Kimberly Boelkes, Principal
Eastview Elementary School
Canton, Illinois

Gwen Gross, Superintendent, Adjunct Professor
Manhattan Beach Unified School District
Manhattan Beach, California

Gail Houghton, Chair, Associate Professor
Department of Educational Leadership
School of Education and Behavioral Studies
Azusa Pacific University
Azusa, California

Ann Porter, 2002 National Distinguished Principal (NAESP)
Lewis & Clark Elementary School
Grand Forks, North Dakota

About the Authors

**Vance Caesar, PhD,** is a Premier Leadership Coach and Mentor, focusing on helping leaders create fulfillment for themselves and their organizations. His clients create more of the life they want while creating the financial results their stakeholders deserve. His extensive background includes being a successful senior executive, entrepreneur, coach, professor, team builder, author, and publisher.

His current clients represent 30 percent of the top 10 fastest-growing companies in the world. His clients include Deloitte & Touche, eBay, Sony, Toyota, Freedom Communications, Boeing, Tenet Healthcare, Conexant, Autobytel, New Century Mortgage, Impac Mortgage, Smith Sport, Broadcom, Procter & Gamble, ITT, Fluidmaster, Taco Bell, Washington Mutual, Foundstone, Sybron Dental Specialties, ADP, SBC, Silverado Senior Living, and Countrywide Mortgage. He is a sought-after resource for World Presidents' Organization (WPO) and Young Presidents' Organization (YPO) chapters and regularly holds weekend retreats for CEOs at his mountain retreat center in Southern California.

His affiliations began as Florida's top Charter President of the U.S. Jaycees in 1969. He has also been on a wide variety of for-profit, nonprofit, and advisory boards. Current affiliations include Founder of the Professional Coaches and Mentors Association; President and Mentor for Orange County's Stanford Business School Alumni Association;

Founder and President of the Young Leader's Organization (YLO); a professor in leadership and entrepreneurism with Pepperdine University for MBA and doctoral candidates; and a board member of Silverado Senior Living, Inc. He has been listed in *Who's Who in America* for more than 30 years and was a regular contributor to the Franklin Covey magazine *Priorities.*

Vance holds a BS degree from The Citadel and a Master's in Business Administration from Florida Atlantic University. He is a graduate of the Stanford University Executive Program, and earned his PhD from Walden University in organizational psychology. His doctoral research was on personality characteristics associated with high-achieving executives who became successful entrepreneurs, 92 percent of whom reported they are not happy. His work over the last decade has emphasized coaching clients to be part of the 8 percent of high achievers who are happy.

Carol Ann Caesar, PhD, works with those who want to create healthier lives. Her clients set priorities and discover paths to help them get to where they want to be, reducing chaos and stress and increasing well-being.

Her extensive background includes being the behavioral scientist at Long Beach Memorial Family Medicine Residency and working in Health Psychology at the Loma Linda Veteran's Hospital. She had a psychology private practice for 15 years, working with hundreds of adults who wanted to create better, healthier lives for themselves. Four years ago, she transitioned into a coaching practice utilizing her background in creating emotional health.

Carol Ann holds a bachelor's degree in education from the University of Florida, a Master's in educational counseling from Florida Atlantic University, a PhD from California School of Professional Psychology (CSPP), and a postdoctoral

Master's from CSPP in clinical psychopharmacology. She is also a certified Authentic Happiness coach. Her dissertation was on the coping beliefs in a myocardial infarct population. High coping beliefs were associated with high self-esteem. In her coaching, she emphasizes the importance of beliefs in people's emotional health.

Introduction

All that is needed to make a happy life is within yourself, in your way of thinking.

—Marcus Aurelius

Our Promise to Readers

We Give You Tools to

- Better understand yourself

- Take away one way to even better get what you want, easier

- Learn what can help you feel fulfilled

- Create your own model for developing more happiness

- Become a more valuable mentor and coach to budding high achievers who also want happiness

Who This Book Is For

This book is for high achievers and those on the path to high achieving who are, or want to be, leading themselves and others.

The Achievers' Dilemma

Our research and observations indicate that less than 10 percent of high achievers feel happy, even with all their accomplishments.

What's It All About?

It's about how you can add happiness and fulfillment to your life, thus becoming a Happy High Achiever.

Happy High Achievers

They are those who continue to higher levels of accomplishment while increasingly liking themselves and experiencing happiness.

Success is getting what you want.

Happiness is wanting what you get.

—Dave Gardner

Where Are You In Your Life?

Are you on the road to achieving your goals? Have you already achieved them and are wondering what the next achievements are going to be? Before pushing further ahead, we hope you will consider what it might take to both achieve and to be happy with your life.

Our research and experience with clients who are high achievers and leaders has brought to light the significant numbers of Americans who are achieving and getting the things they think will make them happy, only to realize that these things all too often result in emptiness and disappointment. We have discovered that only about 10 percent report some degree of happiness.

In studying and observing and coaching leaders from myriad walks of life, we have developed a model that has assisted most of our clients to live more meaningfully happy lives.

We have turned our research and experiences with our clients into the development of this easy-to-read, short book. We know you are busy, with many demands for your attention. We believe the format we have used will help you read through quickly, while offering stops along the way to actually engage yourself in the questions and exercises. It would be easy to skip over these and just read the book. We hope you will take time to ponder and listen intently to yourself. Perhaps you have a coach, a mentor, accountability group, or some other supportive person who has your welfare in the forefront to partner with you.

Suggestions for Reading This Book

We have set up most of the pages on the left-hand side to be a quick summary or statement about the material on the right-hand side, which is more detailed.

The left-hand side helps you go back into the book after reading to get helpful reminders. You can just open the book and review one of the left-hand pages. They can serve you as motivators and reminders of what you have previously read at greater length.

1

Foundations of Achievers

The greatest gift of a life is to spend it for something that will outlast it.

—William James

Our Foundation

High Achievers are:

- Driven

- Responsible

- Confident

- Saddled with shaky self-esteem

Twelve years ago, Vance found himself repeatedly asking the same question. Why is it that some people from similar backgrounds achieve a lot while others do not? After much research and observation, four characteristics of high achievers emerged. From this research, Vance developed his foundation about high achievers.

This foundation is that high achievers are driven, responsible, confident, *and* saddled with shaky self-esteem. Yes, that sounds different than what you probably expect! Let's define our terms.

"Drivenness" is often noticeable as early as age two. We define it as an ability to multi-process while being actively engaged in life because of excitement or fear. Because of this, high achievers are driven to achieve more and more. Drive (or conation) is one of the four domains of human development. The other three are psychomotor/physical, cognitive, and emotional.

Being responsible is holding yourself accountable for what happens in your life. Not being responsible is seeing yourself in a life others create for you. It is orienting on "them," the system, the boss, headquarters, and in general, others. This belief results in reducing yourself to a victim who has little power.

Confidence is the belief that you can do something or learn to do something at least as well as the next person. In short, if anyone else can do it, you believe you also have the energy, drive, and focus to get it done, too. It is a belief in your ability to use your skills and talents to get what you want, and to do what you want to do.

We define self-esteem as your perceived acceptability of self, versus your belief of how acceptable you think or feel you should be.

More About Responsibility

<u>RESPONSIBLE</u>	<u>NOT RESPONSIBLE</u>
I create	Others create
I/me/we*	You, they, them**
Leader	Victim
ILOC***	ELOC****

*   Responsibility-centered conversations use these pronouns.

**   These pronouns are frequently used to blame others.

***   Internal locus of control

****   External locus of control

High achievers take responsibility for their lives.

Taking responsibility for doing, winning, and losing is part of who high achievers are. High achievers speak in terms of "I," "me," and "we."

Are you 100 percent responsible for what happens to you in life? Probably not.

Are you 100 percent responsible for how you respond to what happens to you in life? We believe so. Otherwise, you would see yourself in a life others create for you. Not taking responsibility for yourself is "empowering" yourself into a victim who has no direct power. Usually when people are abdicating personal responsibility for their lives, they use the pronouns "you," "they," and "them."

Taking personal responsibility for what happens in one's life is having an internal locus of control. Believing that forces outside of oneself are pretty much responsible for what happens in one's life is having an external locus of control.

When Vance was in fourth grade, he had a lesson in self-responsibility. Fortunately for him, his teacher, Mrs. White, believed in his ability to learn. She exercised her beliefs about responsibility, which made a difference in his life. The following is their story.

Mrs. White's Story: How Vance Flunked Fourth Grade—Almost

Vance's first three years in elementary school in Miami Springs, Florida, were some of his happiest. He had friends, excelled at physical education, and felt loved.

Vance's reading and spelling weren't particularly strong. He did everything he could to avoid reading aloud in class because of the snickers he'd hear from his classmates.

His second- and third-grade teachers had passed him, probably mostly out of compassion and a belief that holding him back would negatively impact his self-esteem. He was learning that he did not have to be responsible for learning to read and spell.

When he arrived in Mrs. White's fourth-grade class, he very quickly was given an opportunity to learn something about his responsibility to learn. The fifth week of school, Mrs. White sent a note home suggesting a speedily held parent conference.

During the conference, Mrs. White told Vance's mother and the principal that Vance should be put back into third grade because he wasn't even close to reading or spelling at grade level. Since he was the youngest in the class, being put back wouldn't be such a bad thing.

Vance's mother cried. Vance was embarrassed and afraid. He started crying, too. Between sobs he asked for one more chance to show he belonged in Mrs. White's class. She agreed to work with him after school four days a week for six weeks. If after that he wasn't progressing satisfactorily, he'd be put back into a third-grade class.

Mrs. White also expected Vance to work at home on assignments that she would give him. It would require that he put his best efforts and attention to the tasks.

Vance remembers growing up a lot during those six weeks. He even took upon himself the responsibility of seeking out extra help from his grandmother. He practiced reading and learning to spell words with her.

Mrs. White also kept her promise to be responsible for the extra time and attention Vance needed to begin to catch up.

Vance learned

- To be responsible for his own learning;
- To take school more seriously;
- To be grateful for the opportunity to be responsible for his own results by working harder and smarter;
- That there were people who really loved him enough to be interested in his growth.

On the next page is a statement for you to consider about personal responsibility and opportunity.

A Quiz

Carefully consider the following statement, and then decide on your response.

I've always done the most important thing for me to do, at that time, given the information I had at that time.

Now decide if you believe this statement to be true or false.

TRUE _____   FALSE _____

Answer the quiz on the opposite page with true or false, whichever is "your truth."

Don't read further until you have answered this for yourself, based on your reflection of your beliefs and behaviors, not your intended behaviors.

This question is not addressing what you *should* have done or what was *best* for you to have done. It is simply a question asking what your belief is about your choices and your responsibility for them.

> *Nobody's problem is ideal. Nobody has things just as they would like them. The thing to do is to make a success with what material I have. It is sheer waste of time and soul-power to imagine what I would do if things were different. They are not different.*
>
> —Dr. Frank Crane

A Quiz

> *I've always done the most important thing for me to do, at that time, given the information I had at the time.*

TRUE __X__   FALSE _____

We believe that everyone does what is most important for them to do, at that time, given the information they had at the time of the decision.

> *Every successful person I have heard of has done the best they could with conditions as they found them, and not waited until the next year for better.*
>
> —Edgar Watson Howe

This quiz comes from our understanding of Viktor Frankl's writings in his well-known book, *Man's Search for Meaning*. As a prisoner in Auschwitz and other camps, he knew that there were some people who were immediately killed by people and events beyond their control. Of the remaining people, himself included, he eventually believed there was a choice made about how each would respond to the reprehensible conditions. He came to believe that each prisoner retained his or her free choice of how to view the events in his or her life and to choose to do what was most important to him or her at that time.

When high achievers believe this statement is true for them, they give themselves at least three powerful gifts:

1. They conclude their life is reflective of decisions they have made to date, empowering them to consider choices for the future.

2. They are optimizing their learning from the consequences of each of their decisions.

3. They have the key to forgiveness in their hands, creating light and "liteness," shedding blame, and increasing self-esteem.

More About Confidence

- **Situational**

- **"I can learn to do that"**

- **"I can do that"**

Faith in your own powers and confidence in your individual methods are essential to success.

—Roderick Stevens

Confidence is a belief that one can learn to do something, or one already knows how to do something, in a particular situation or activity.

An example of confidence is when a pilot feels certain of being able to fly a particular type of airplane at a particular time. Even a veteran pilot may lack confidence in flying a plane in certain conditions. A nonpilot probably wouldn't feel as confident to fly a plane as the pilot.

Confidence and self-esteem are not the same. Confidence is situation-specific, and self-esteem is a pervasive way people feel about their worthiness and acceptability.

The self-esteem of the pilot and the nonpilot are not predictable just because of the level of confidence they have in piloting a plane. The nonpilot might feel confident about some other skill, such as teaching 20 first graders.

More About Self-Esteem

Self-esteem and confidence are different.

$$\frac{\text{Perceived Acceptablity}}{\text{Belief of How I Should Be}} = \text{Self-Esteem}$$

How acceptable I feel I am versus how I am.

> *The pious and just honoring of ourselves may be thought the fountainhead from whence every laudable and worthy enterprise issues forth.*
>
> —John Milton

The secret that many high achievers probably like to keep to themselves is that they are saddled with low self-esteem.* Yep. They often say to themselves, "I should be better, richer, liked by more people, and have a better body." The operative word is "should." It drives you to hurdling over bars you set higher and higher . . . keeping you striving and striving and striving to achieve more, more, and more.

This phenomenon is referred to as the "hungry ghost" in the Buddhist tradition. It has a huge stomach and a very small mouth. Nothing fills up the hungry ghost within, no matter how continuous the stream of "goodies." The amount put in rarely registers on the fuel gauge. It is like trying to fill a bucket with a hole in the bottom. It fuels a constant need to do more, acquire more, be more.

Yes, there is value in low self-esteem if you care about achieving more, more, and more!

In *Fast Company* magazine (1999), Tom Morris distinguishes between an unhealthy "dissatisfaction of acquisition" versus a healthy "dissatisfaction of aspiration." The former centers on having more "things"; The latter centers on who you want to become, setting up growth to be more effective and more loving while expanding your horizons.

The combination of low self-esteem with high drive, confidence, and self-responsibility is jet fuel, powering a highly accomplished life.

---

*There are many ways to measure self-esteem. We have used the Coopersmith Inventory with high achievers and found that they are in about the 10th percentile. This means that about 90 percent of people taking this inventory have higher self-esteem scores!

Review

The High Achiever's Profile:

- High drive

- High responsibility

- High confidence

- Low self-esteem

Let's review.

The high achiever's profile includes being driven, responsible, confident, and saddled with shaky self-esteem. Are you one of them?

Based on our research, there is a problem for many high achievers: only about 1 in 10 reports being happy.

After Vance finished his doctoral dissertation, he had an instinct that the high achievers in his study were not happy with their lives. Although this was counterintuitive to our cultural belief, he recalled the repeated interviews he had with community and business leaders, celebrities, astronauts, and Olympic champions. He decided to do a follow-up study.

His study of 100 high achievers resulted in 92 percent rating themselves with some degree of unhappiness. The past decade has confirmed these data as Vance has worked with thousands of high-achieving educators, graduate students, corporate executives, pastors, and business owners in one-on-one coaching and group sessions worldwide. His original results are reinforced daily. About 1 in 10 high achievers in myriad walks of life rates him- or herself with some degree of happiness.

Those 8 percent began to be our teachers. They can now also be yours, by our sharing what we have learned these last 10 years.

The Problem

Ninety-two percent of high achievers are not happy!

How sad that so few of these achievers are Happy High Achievers!

It seems to us that a big part of life is creating happiness for oneself. We wondered what was at the root of the happiness experienced by the 8 percent.

We even began to ask ourselves, "Why strive to be a high achiever unless there is a way to also be happy?" Why would anyone want to be a high achiever if 9 out of 10 were not happy?

We decided to discover what makes the difference between the high achievers who are not happy and those who are happy.

All leadership begins with self-leadership.

—Noah benShea

What Can We Learn From Happy High Achievers?

> *The road to happiness lies in two simple principles:*
>
> *Find what it is that interests you and that you do well, and when you find it, put your whole soul into it—every bit of energy and ambition and natural ability you have.*
>
> —John D. Rockefeller

Our focus is

1. Getting to know the 8 percent of high achievers who are happy;

2. Learning to borrow the wisdom of Happy High Achievers (HHAs) for our own growth and to be better able to serve others in their journey toward happiness and achievement.

Leadership and learning are indispensable to each other.

—John F. Kennedy

Happy High Achievers' Life Model

I. Purpose

II. Vision

III. Meaningful work

IV. Relationships → energy

V. Beliefs and behaviors → peace

VI. Three R's: Review, renew, and recommit

VII. Discipline

We have observed that happy high-achieving Americans have a powerfully simple life model.

We have seen pieces of this model in myriad ancient writings of many kinds. These pieces keep showing up in psychology books as well as in spiritual and self-help publications. Why? Because they make such simple sense and hold true over the centuries.

We have integrated these pieces into a cohesive, comprehensive, comprehensible model. It is one that can easily guide you in your efforts to both achieve and to feel happy with yourself and your life.

Let's begin our exploration of the seven keys that, when utilized together holistically, have transformed so many people into Happy High Achievers.

The very essence of leadership is that you have to have a vision.

—Theodore Hesburgh

A Real-Life Example

Naomi Judd strikes us as a classic example of a high achiever who became a Happy High Achiever. She shared some of her story and her wisdom in the February 8, 2004, issue of *American Profile.*

Judd was at a low point in her life. It was a time when she didn't feel worthy. She was a young, single mother with two children, no money, no education, and no resources. She felt trapped and overwhelmed. In a flash, she realized that her desperate situation was a result of all the small and large inappropriate choices she had been making and which had shaped her life.

Naomi Judd called on her beliefs and behaviors to reverse the course of her life. She realized that she was not bad and that she could work her way out of these dire circumstances.

She had plenty of drive. She worked as a waitress while earning a nursing degree. She also kept alive a dream. She had a vision of being a star, of writing a number one song and winning a Grammy for Songwriter of the Year. She had a belief that "You become whatever you think about all day." She eventually won that Grammy.

She realized that the success and money were not the keys to her happiness. She chose not to participate in materialism. She developed practices to find peace of mind. She chose to begin each day with 20 minutes of solitude, which helped her reduce stress and improve her health. She examined what truly made her happy and followed that path.

Naomi Judd also found her true calling. She realizec she could use her own life story, sharing the choices she n and their consequences, to help others. She has written a book about what she has learned on her life's journey, *Naomi's Breakthrough Guide: 20 Choices to Transform Your Life.*

Naomi is candid about her belief in her ability to control her choices and reactions to what circumstances occur in her life. She states, "Peace of mind isn't the absence of problems; peace of mind comes from your ability to deal with them. The more we understand ourselves and what's standing in the way of our being as happy and healthy as we can, and the more eager we become to risk following our dreams and offering our gifts to others, the more worthy we feel, the more we choose peace of mind."

2

Purpose

I don't know what your destiny will be, but one thing I do know. The only ones among you who will be really happy are those who have sought and found how to serve.

—Albert Schweitzer

What Is Purpose?

- Beingness

- A context for living our lives

- The "why" or reason we exist

- What we are meant to do at this time of our lives

- Something bigger than ourselves

- Something that defines how we see life each day

- A way of using our strengths to serve others

- Our soul's work

The first key of the Happy High Achiever model is discovering and clearly articulating your life purpose at this phase in your life.

We live in a time in which institutions may be able to protect us from hunger, thirst, and cold. But they will not be able to airlift us out of the misery resulting from absence of purpose and ignorance of how to use purpose to change our lives and others'.

Having clarity of purpose helps to create success and abundance. These are not separate things to "get" but are part of a person's whole being and attitude. This is a concept with ancient roots, and is not about assuming that success alone creates abundance.

In religious circles, we'd say those with clarity of purpose are clear about their calling. In business and education circles, we'd say they are clear about their mission statement. High-functioning and happy organizations (gatherings of individuals) have clarity of their mission. They use this to unify each other and all their associates and clients toward better serving the world.

Whether you call it a mission, a purpose, or a calling, it is the answer to the questions, "Why am I here?" "What is it that I do or can do that makes a difference in the world?"

You can give yourself these answers, too. It is already in you. It changes as you grow and change, too.

Let's review some purpose statements.

Examples of Purpose

- To be the <u>happiest</u> place on earth (Disneyland)

- To <u>serve</u> each customer as we meet/exceed their expectations every time by using our common sense (Nordstrom)

- To serve my higher power by coaching successful <u>leaders</u> toward their creating more <u>joyful</u> purpose and fulfillment in their lives, and their doing the same for others (Vance Caesar)

- To give <u>unlimited opportunity</u> to women (Mary Kay Cosmetics)

- To live each day so my five children can say with love and respect, <u>"That's my Dad!"</u> (CEO, commercial real estate company)

- To <u>preserve and improve</u> human life (Merck)

- To <u>give ordinary folk</u> the chance to buy the same things as rich people (Wal-Mart)

Note Disneyland's purpose. There are six amusement parks in Southern California. None has as high pricing, long lines, and mediocre rides as does Disneyland. And none has as many people paying to enjoy these high prices, long lines, and mediocre rides. Why? We believe it is because Disneyland is the only one among its competitors with clarity of purpose that is shared by every employee, from the parking lot attendant to the last person we see sweeping up the smallest pieces of paper . . . all toward creating for each guest an experience of being part of the happiest place on earth.

People are attracted to a purpose and to those who have purpose!

Disneyland's purpose is clear. It is so clear it can be summarized by one word. That word? "Happiest."

When an organization or individual has purpose, they attract others, including talented personnel and loyal customers and resources. You, too, can begin to identify your purpose or reason for "being" at this phase of your life.

We will help you get started with the following. But for a more in-depth look at this subject, we refer you to two of the many books we like on discovering your purpose. One is *The Path* by Laurie Beth Jones. The other is *Leadership from the Inside Out* by Kevin Cashman, who makes these statements about purpose: "Purpose is life flowing through us," "Purpose releases energy," and "Purpose is bigger and deeper than our goals."

Words-in-the-Box

- Happiest

- To serve

- Joyful leaders

- Unlimited opportunity

- That's my Dad!

- Preserve/improve life

The concept of a "word-in-the-box" comes from the story of Coca-Cola's introduction of New Coke.

It seems, following New Coke's introduction, its sales and the sales of other Coca-Cola products shrank at a scary rate—so scary that Coke's board of directors called an emergency board meeting in Atlanta. The marketing facilitator, as Vance heard the story told, asked the board to start their meeting with a review of the company's mission statement, which he had written on the white board in the company's boardroom. Then he drew a box above the mission statement, asking the board to place in the box one word that describes or summarizes the company's mission or purpose. Words like tradition, real, and heritage emerged from the discussion.

He chose the word "tradition" to write in the box. The board agreed.

With Coca-Cola's word-in-the-box being tradition, the facilitator asked, "What do you want to do with New Coke?" The decision on the future of New Coke was easy: scuttle it.

A huge financial decision was made easy. Why? Because New Coke was a concept that did not align with the company's mission or purpose: tradition.

The board then decided to replace New Coke. They wanted no empty shelves in the beverage sections of your local grocery stores. What to replace New Coke with was also easy.

Classic Coke was born out of the clarity of purpose provided by Coke's word-in-the-box exercise.

It's the same in our lives. With clarity of purpose, other decisions come easier and faster.

Create Your Word-in-the-Box

```
┌─────────────────────┐
│                     │
│                     │
└─────────────────────┘
```

> *All the world over it is true that a double-minded person is unstable in all his ways, like a wave on the streamlet, tossed hither and thither, with every eddy of its tide. A determinate purpose in life and a steady adhesion to it through all disadvantages, are indispensable conditions of success.*
>
> —William M. Punshon

Now it's your turn. Having clarity of purpos
creating a fulfilling life, organization, or famil
word-in-the-box is a first step toward developing you
pose statement.

What could be your personal word-in-the-box at this stage
of your life?

What is the one word that first comes into your mind? Is it
something you love to do? Is it a verb? Verbs often used in
mission statements include the following:

Serve	Propel	Create
Help	Lead	Heal
Rally	Improve	Teach
Encourage	Give	Share

After deciding on your word-in-the-box, consider adding
other words to it toward creating your purpose. Can you
think of one word? What is it?

If you can think of one word and then a second, a third,
and a fourth, you are well on your way to creating a purpose
statement. It only takes one sentence to frame the purpose of
your life!

What is your personal and/or professional word-in-the-
box?

Reminder: It's the core of your purpose.

An Application of Purpose

- **For whom are you living your life?**

- **For whom would you like to live your life?**

- **What are the implications?**

Next, let's add another component by asking those to whom you are normally giving your a.. consciousness . . . or in other words, your life! Said simp₁y, whom are you living?

As you look at your calendar the past 60 days, you'll get a hint. But that's not the whole story. The whole story is your assessment of to whom you have given your awareness and consciousness. Who was first, second, third, and even last?

Where on the list is your spouse or partner? How about your children, parents, siblings, friends, and neighbors? How about your bosses, clients, or employees? Where are you on the list? Who or what else is on your list?

Look at your list . . . look at it. Is it serving you well? If yes, how can you maintain it?

If you want to change the order of to whom you are giving your life (attention and consciousness), how would you like your life list to be?

I would like my life list to be

You now have the verb (or action) and the noun (or whom you serve) of your purpose statement. Congratulations!

3

Vision

Happy are those who dream dreams and are ready to pay the price to make them come true.

—Leon J. Suenens

Believe in your strength and your vision.

—André Gide

Vision

(Something You See)

- The "what" that success looks like

- Your goals and your milestones along the way

- Content we can see that is often measurable, tangible, and time-defined versus the context (purpose)

If one advances confidently in the direction of his dreams, and endeavors to live the life which he has imagined, he will meet with a success unexpected in common hours.

—Henry David Thoreau

Having a vision is the second key.

Knowing where you are going is crucial to getting there the easy way. Otherwise, you confuse activity with accomplishment.

Vance relates, "There are many times I have found myself driving somewhat over the speed limit, happy with the pace at which we are making progress, when Carol Ann has asked, 'Where are we going?' I sheepishly have answered that I don't know, but we're making great time. I remember, then, that getting to where I want to go starts with knowing where I want to be. It has been most helpful to be able to have a mental picture of that destination."

Having a vision of your destination (with milestones along the way) gives you power. Your vision is something measurable and tangible. You can see it in your mind. The more specific, the better the vision is. There are dates by which you want to achieve milestones toward the vision, and even a date by which you want to achieve the goal or the vision.

Often when Vance speaks, he shares his vision. We'll share it with you, also. He can see Carol Ann's 80th birthday. Our grandchildren have baked a birthday cake rather than running by a bakery at the last minute. Our family and close friends have come together at our beach home for a party and have enjoyed lunch and cake. After our guests have left, we walk hand in hand out to the beach for the half-mile walk in the sand to the pier. We enjoy the view from the pier. We walk the half mile back to our home.

Examples of Vision

- Hold hands with my wife on a mile walk after her 80th birthday party hosted by our grandchildren at our beach home, and they baked the cake. (Vance Caesar)

- Have our software in every home, car, and office within the next decade. (Microsoft)

- Have 1 million guests pay to visit the next 60 days with each taking away an experience so positive they share it often and enthusiastically. (Disneyland)

- Become the Harvard of the West. (Stanford)

The first example of vision is Vance's. It assumes the following:

1. We've shared in our grandchildrens' lives to where they want to bake the cake.

2. We're healthy enough to walk a mile in the sand.

3. We can afford to live on the beach.

4. We love each other enough to want to hold hands.

A great story about vision is Walt Disney's insistence that Disney World's castle be built before the rest of the Orlando, Florida, park. Why? So the road builders, the parking lot pavers, the contractors creating Main Street, and the rest of Disney World could see the heart of the park years before anyone could attend. Disney wanted to create a tangible vision for all to see of what this special part of his dream looked like . . . in spite of the millions of extra dollars it cost to build the castle first.

"We made up the extra cost to build the castle first within the first year," Walt reportedly said following Disney World's opening in 1971.

Walt wanted each worker and millions of future guests to see the castle years before the grand opening because he knew the power of creating a vision others could see and share. Walt was a genius.

What is your castle? What is your vision for five years from now? How about for your 90th birthday party? Have you shared your vision with others who can help you create it?

Every professor of leadership we know agrees that a leader creates a vision and enrolls others in it. Well, we think leadership of others starts with leadership of self. Therefore, in what vision have you enrolled yourself?

Easy Ways to
Create Your Vision

Answer these four questions:

1. What do I want to feel?

2. What do I want to do?

3. What do I want to own?

4. What do I want to contribute?

One easy way to create a vision is to answer four core questions: what do I want to feel, what do I want to do, what do I want to own, and what do I want to contribute (some call this "legacy").

Put each question at the top of a blank page. Give yourself at least three separate sittings to fully answer each question. Write down the possibilities. Give yourself time to dream and to listen to your inner longings. You can always delete.

Next, select your most important two or three answers for each of the four questions. Then, for the next 90 days, center your life on creating the two feelings most important to you to create. Some possibilities are fulfillment, excitement, adventure, peace, healthiness, balance, growth, love, abundance, and spirituality.

Then assure that what you do, what you own, and how you serve others contributes to creating those feelings you most want in your life.

Challenge yourself to alter or say no to doing anything that conflicts with your goal of having the two feelings you have committed to creating in your life. Say no to buying or keeping things that are not in alignment with your creating those feelings you want. Maybe now is the time to discard things that conflict with how you want to feel. Say yes to the parts of your life that result in the feelings you desire.

Contributing to others is a wonderful way to create abundance in your life. Doing it with focus on your visualized core feelings gives you more power to create the life you really want.

More About Creating Vision

Discover Your Life Vision Through Pictures

Your River of Life Picture

The first picture is what you see when you answer the following questions: If you were on a river right now, what would it look like? Would it be a fast-changing river with crosscurrents, falls, and suck holes? Would it have high walls of granite? Or would it be a wide, peaceful Mississippi River with low, gentle banks inviting lazy respites along the way? Are there any people other than you in the picture? How are they interacting with you? What is your role? Or are no others to be seen?

What does your boat look like? Does it feel safe? Do you have a destination? What is it? How will you get there? How do you feel in this picture?

Take time to really see your picture in detail, or better yet, draw it with all the color and boldness you can muster. It's your picture of yourself on the river of life as you may be experiencing life today. Now take a break for at least five minutes.

Returning from your break, create a second picture. It's you back on your river in 20 years. What do you want to create? Who's with you? What's the boat like? How about the river, the weather, and the feelings and stories shared between others? Is it a colorful picture? Is there a destination? Is it in alignment with how you want to feel?

As you draw your second river picture with even more gusto than the first, keep in mind what it is that you really want to have in your life. Keep your picture where you see it frequently, maybe on the wall next to your desk, on your refrigerator, or in your calendar. Vance likes to put his on the garage wall, where the lights of his car illuminate his "future" picture as he leaves and returns home daily.

Let your subconscious go to work. It is a powerhouse of creativity, working many times faster and longer each day than your conscious mind. Once your subconscious "gets it" that this is your vision, it is focused on helping you create it.

Your River of Life Now

Your River of Life in 20 Years

More About Creating Vision

YOUR Life Stories

Another way to enlist the powerhouse of your subconscious is to write the life stories today you want told at your 90th birthday party, or perhaps at your funeral. That's right, write the life stories now, the way *you* want them told, versus waiting for someone else to write them the way they want your life stories told.

An easy way to write your stories is to use the answers to four sets of questions. The questions are

1. What do you want said about your role in your family, as a son or daughter, spouse, mother or father, grandmother or grandfather, uncle or aunt, etc.? What did you contribute to your family? What role did you play in others' lives as they grew? Were you known for contributing something unique? What and why?

2. What do you want said about your role in your profession? Did you contribute? With whom were your relationships? How did people talk about you and the results you created?

3. What do you want said about you as a neighbor and member of your community? What did you contribute or take away? In what way was your community better because you lived there?

4. What message do you leave about your values and beliefs and how you have made decisions along the way?

Keep your story to 200–300 words. Keep them succinct and visible. Allow your subconscious powerhouse to work, collaborating with your efforts to make the stories come true.

Your Answers to
Four Sets of Questions

Question 1:

Question 2:

Question 3:

Question 4:

Your Life Story

More About Creating Vision

Your Ideal 14 Days

Here is a fourth technique for creating your vision. Put a blank calendar in front of yourself. Select 14 consecutive days three years from now, or maybe around a special birthday, say your 50th or 65th. Then begin to fill in each day on your ideal calendar with what you most want to have in your life.

As you begin to fill in your calendar, consider the following questions to help you get started: With whom do you have breakfast, and what do you talk about? How about lunch? Where will you be, and with whom? What activities do you most want to include in your afternoon? How will the daylight end, and what will you be doing in the evening? With whom? Post everything.

Then, take a look at your ideal 14 days and keep them visible. Again, the powerhouse of your subconscious now has some specifics that can kick it into gear and probably create it more easily than you ever believed.

As you are fully engaging in these vision-creating activities, keep in mind that the only comparisons being made are with yourself. Where were you yesterday and last year in becoming who you are? This is not a contest where you measure yourself against other people or others' expectations.

Ideal 14 Days

Day 1

Day 2

Day 3

Day 4

Day 5

Day 6

Day 7

Day 8

Day 9

Day 10

Day 11

Day 12

Day 13

Day 14

Vision Under the Most Extreme Conditions

Viktor Frankl's description of his vision while being held prisoner in Auschwitz is tangible.

Since 1989, when we read Viktor Frankl's book, *Man's Search for Meaning*, we have been struck by the power in having a clear, tangible vision. He was a psychiatrist in Austria at the outbreak of World War II.

As mentioned earlier, Viktor Frankl and his family were victims of the Holocaust. His family was killed soon after arriving at the camp at Auschwitz. Frankl was put to work under the most horrifying and degrading circumstances.

Frankl determined that if he was not murdered, he would work on three goals. His first goal was to survive. The second was to help others through his medical training. The third was to learn something.

While working on his goals and helping others, Dr. Frankl had the realization of a vision of the future for himself. He was able to visualize himself in a beautiful, well-appointed, and warm auditorium lecturing to people in upholstered chairs on the psychology of the concentration camp.

Frankl had observed that, of the people not killed outright, those who survived had a vision of something left to achieve in their lives that no one else could do. This does not mean that everyone who had a vision survived—just that those who did survive had some sort of vision for the future. They were able to live in and focus on the moment while also creating thoughts that would form their future.

The take-home point for us is how powerful having a tangible vision can be. By the way, his vision came true. We remember that he went on to be the lead speaker at a world-wide psychological convention, telling of his life and the lessons he learned in it. He also taught at five universities in the United States and received numerous honorary degrees. He lived to be 92 years old.

4

Meaningful Work

I know what happiness is, for I have done good work.

—Robert Louis Stevenson

To find a career to which you are adapted by nature, and then to work hard at it, is about as near to a formula for success and happiness as the world provides. One of the fortunate aspects of this formula is that, granted the right career has been found, the hard work takes care of itself. Then hard work is not hard work at all.

—Mark Sullivan

Meaningful Work*

- Your work is in integrity with your purpose. There is a higher purpose for your work!

- Your work is getting you to your goals, to your vision.

The persons who will use their skill and constructive imagination to see how much they can give for a dollar, instead of how little they can give for a dollar, are bound to succeed.

—Henry Ford

---

*You'll never have to go to "work" again when you've created this!

The third key to being a Happy High Achiever involves creating work that is so full of meaning that you never have to go to "work." Your work is your life, and your life is your work, just like Mother Teresa, Bill Gates, Princess Diana, and probably Jimmy Carter in his later years.

Jimmy Carter seems to have created work through Habitat for Humanity where he wins . . . where his work is aligned with his purpose. Work can fulfill your purpose, making a difference of which you are aware. That's the key.

Tom Morris states, "Successful people work to discover their talents, to develop those talents, and then to use those talents to benefit others as well as themselves."

The three bricklayers' story below illustrates meaningful work that utilizes talents to give something to self and to others. The third bricklayer finds meaning and something bigger than himself in the work that he does. We have heard this story told somewhat differently on several occasions, without there ever being an author attributed to it. Several years ago we saw the story told in a book of inspirational quotes, again with no author attributed to the story. The following is our version of the idea.

Meaningful Work

- When your work is in integrity with your purpose, there is meaningfulness.

- When there is meaningfulness, you attract more resources.

- People are attracted to you and see you as a true leader.

"The Three Bricklayers"
Story

I look on that person as happy who, when there is a question of success, looks into his work for a reply.

—Ralph Waldo Emerson

A famous architect was anonymously touring the site of a great cathedral he had designed. Observing three bricklayers, he asked the first one, "What are you doing?" The first bricklayer replied, "I'm making enough money to pay the rent. I'll be glad when the day and the week are over and Friday arrives." With resentment and heaviness, the first bricklayer works each day to get by.

The second bricklayer is doing the same work and answers the same question, saying, "I am waiting for the time I can be happy. I'll have a better job, a better boss and coworkers. Meanwhile, I'm just going through the motions to get through each day. Some day I'll retire, and then I'll do what I really want to do."

The third bricklayer, when asked, "What are you doing?" says, "We're all building a cathedral here. What a privilege it will be to ride by it each day the rest of my days here on earth and see the contribution I have made to our community and our world. I love laying bricks!"

The third bricklayer has an advantage—actually, plenty of advantages. These include more job opportunities with the freedom to choose from these multiple offers; more people who want to be direct reports; getting more done with less effort; being healthier and happier.

At age 65, upon retirement, the third bricklayer plans to lay bricks with Habitat for Humanity so that "I can contribute to creating houses for families who wouldn't have had them. What a way to give back to a life that has given me so much." Bricklayer three gets "paid" plenty and is a Happy High Achiever.

Which are you? The first, second, or third bricklayer? How do you describe yourself at the end of each day? How do others describe you?

What Happens When Work Is Meaningful

- You become an irresistible attraction.

- You have advantages.

- There is inspiration and motivation.

- Self-leadership is evident.

- You get paid plenty!

The Byron Harless Lesson

Getting paid plenty is our responsibility. The following story is about how Vance learned this crucial point.

Three weeks after I joined Knight Newspapers as a freshly minted MBA, I found myself staring at our vice-chairman, Byron Harless, as he walked into my office at 9:00 p.m. Friday. "Why are you still at your desk? You were in the office at 7:15 this morning. And don't you have a briefing with the executive committee Monday morning?" he asked.

I said, "Yes Byron, I do have a briefing, and I am at my desk because I want to be prepared. In fact, I plan to be working this weekend."

Byron then asked me, "Vance, if you resigned from Knight Newspapers tonight, do you feel you've given more than you've gotten?"

"Yes!" I said in a flash. "And that is what I think it takes to establish myself as a high-potential executive who might have a chance to be CEO here someday," I answered.

Standing there in his black-tie outfit, with his face becoming red, he looked like the all-American quarterback he had been at the University of Florida who had just learned his receiver had dropped a perfect Hail Mary pass for the championship. "See me in my office at 8:00 Monday morning, an hour before your scheduled briefing with the executive committee. And don't be late!" he barked.

As Byron whirled around, I realized I had given him the wrong answer.

I didn't sleep well that weekend. I wasn't going to change my answer, though, because I knew I was right. I had given a lot more to the company during my first three weeks on the job.

Monday morning at 8:00, I was knocking at his door. "Come in and don't even sit down," he said grumpily. He stood up and asked me again, "Vance, do you really feel you have given more to this company than you have gotten during the first three weeks on the job as our investor relations contact and as the administrative assistant to the president?"

"Yes Byron," I said confidently. "Well you *better* have a different answer at 5:00 this afternoon," he said as intensely and sharply. "You're dismissed," I heard as he turned his back on me. I left his office shaken.

As I talked to Hal Jurgensmeyer, the president of The Miami Herald Publishing Company and my official boss, about that morning's "conversation" and what had happened Friday evening, Hal asked me to have a seat and think about how I could answer Byron's question differently and stay in integrity.

Hal asked me if I had gotten value out of my position for the last three weeks in terms of the following: "Have you been paid fairly? Have you learned a lot and felt like you've grown? Have you met people who energize you and others you've connected with who could empower you to do even more for others? Have you had fun? Has your job opened for you new life choices and access to myriad parts of society? Do you feel you have begun to make a difference? And, does working here strengthen your reputation or your personal brand?"

My answer to all seven questions was yes! I had been financially fairly paid $12,500 annually and provided a basic benefit program. I had learned more than I ever thought I could learn in three weeks. I had been able to apply almost everything I was exposed to during my MBA program and had learned huge amounts about the First Amendment and its role in our society.

I had made contacts with many of the American media elite. Katharine Graham had even asked her son Don to spend some time with me to learn about newspaper operations in what then was the most technologically advanced metropolitan newspaper in the world, The Miami Herald. I had already met Al Neuharth (chair of Gannett Newspapers and the father of USA Today), CEOs of at least a dozen newspaper and TV groups, plus some of the best teachers in the media.

I had fun. What a great feeling I had walking into the press room at midnight and seeing our six huge presses spewing out thousands of newspapers a minute that would impact millions of people's lives.

I was realizing the many choices beginning to materialize in my life. I had been able to make a difference in people's lives. I said to Hal, "I took this job with your commitment that we would not lay off anyone as we introduced new technology. You have held up your end of the bargain as we have planned to eliminate hundreds of production positions as a result of introducing technology throughout *The Miami Herald's* production division. All of these things are creating a reputation for myself."

Hal suggested I consider all seven answers as currencies when responding to Byron this afternoon. Money, knowledge and growth, relationships, fun, life choices, legacy, and reputation all had value, like any currency.

I stared at Hal. What a concept to include all these commodities in my pay picture. After I broke my silence, I responded, "Yes! I have gotten a lot more than I have given during the last three weeks." Hal then suggested that at 5:00 I try that answer with Byron.

At 4:58 p.m., I was knocking on Byron's door. He invited me in and very sternly said, "Don't even sit down unless you've changed your answer."

I said, "Byron, I have changed my answer, and I've done it with a lot of thoughtfulness. I am happy with my answer."

Getting Paid Plenty

Currencies include

- Money

- Knowledge and growth

- Relationships that give you energy and that give you power

- Fun

- Life choices you want

- Legacy

- Reputation and brand

Byron asked me to sit down across the desk from where he was seated in his large executive suite overlooking Biscayne Bay in Miami. "Why have you changed your answer?" he asked with skepticism. I told him about the seven currencies and how I knew I was getting a lot more than I was giving, and that I appreciated tremendously the opportunity to be at Knight Newspapers.

Byron then very intentionally pulled a white sheet of paper out of the top left-hand drawer of his desk and slid it across the desk surface to me. He said that it was my resignation letter! I looked at it with my hands noticeably shaking. I asked why he had just given me my resignation letter. He said he wasn't going to ask me to sign it this time because I had the right answer.

As he took it back from my trembling hands and slid it into its home space in his desk drawer, he said, "Vance, if at any time you feel you are not getting more than you are giving on this job, you will have done something that is usually irreversible. You will have planted the seed of resentment. Once the seed of resentment is planted into your head, you will look for evidence that supports your feeling resentful. If you look hard enough, you will find plenty of evidence to be resentful. That seed will have sprouted and grown into a huge tree over your head, casting a shadow that will increasingly darken your experience here. The tree's roots will have deepened to where you will be experiencing deeply seated resentment throughout your career. That resentment can cost Knight Newspapers a lot of money. If you feel that your job is an opportunity, and it fills you with gratitude, then we are doing the right thing, and so are you! If at any time that is not the truth, then I am going to pull out your letter of resignation and ask you to sign it immediately. Do you understand?"

"Getting" More Than You "Give"

It is an attitude.

It is a belief.

It is your responsibility.

Man cannot be satisfied with mere success. He is concerned with the terms upon which success comes to him. And very often the terms seem more important than the success.

—Charles A. Bennett

The next 18 years of my career at Knight Newspapers, and then Ridder Newspapers, Byron was my coach. Each time he saw me at a conference or met with me in a coaching session or called me, one of the first questions he would ask was, "Are you getting more than you are giving?" We both knew what the answer needed to be. I understood the contract. He was responsible for assuring that I got more than I gave, and I was responsible for making sure that I got more than I gave. It was a partnership.

This lesson is one that has permeated my contextual view of all relationships. Whether they include my marriage of 38 years, my relationships with clients, or those with business associates, I have always driven to make sure I "get" more than I "give." How? By giving in a way that I am able to optimize each of the seven currencies.

You can use this idea, too. We will explore this further in the next chapter using our get/give scoreboard. It is a simple matrix, which allows you to take a look at what you are giving and what you are getting in each key relationship in your life. We encourage you to consider it as a tool, to help you get more than you ever imagined.

For Happy High Achievers, Meaningful Work Leads to Achieving Purpose and Vision

Get To's and Got To's Story

Create More "Get To's" Than "Got To's"

More people will want to be around you.

You will be more energized.

Work is meaningful when it is getting you to your goals and vision. Activity without a destination can easily turn into flailing, fatigue, and impending burnout. Purposeful work, work that rewards you with energy and a sense of destiny, is a true blessing that is within your grasp every day. The following are two stories for examples.

Harold Lannom, Vance's high school football coach, wanted each player to play his perfect position on the Hialeah High School (Florida) team. During sophomore tryouts, he told each player, "Your ideal job on this team is the job that mirrors, as perfectly as we can create, the person who holds it. That's why our coaching staff wants to get to know you on and off the field. That's why we'll ask questions about your nonfootball hobbies and your beliefs about yourself and your role while in high school."

Coach Lannom and his staff kept asking those questions all three years Vance played football. Yes, Vance had an "ideal" job as the running back. More importantly, he learned much about himself and how to create meaningful work for himself and others, thanks to Coach Lannom's work-person matching techniques. We see this same phenomenon in high-performing schools and companies today.

We especially see this matching occurring in workplaces that look for people's strengths and match strengths to task. For more about this, we refer you to books like *Now, Discover Your Strengths* by Marcus Buckingham and Donald O. Clifton.

In another football lesson, Vance is reminded of his third day of freshman football practice at The Citadel, where he was on a football scholarship. He relates the following story.

It was a typical hot, steamy August day in Charleston, South Carolina. I walked, head drooping, onto the practice field. I'd become bruised and beat up from running plays for the first-string defense as they practiced knocking the heck out of the opposing running back (me).

"Where ya headin', Caesar?" said Jack Hall, the freshman coach, in his distinctive southern drawl.

"Got to go to practice, coach," I replied. The softness of the exchange snapped to tension as he turned into the drill instructor he was in another life.

He barked, "Get over here on the double, cadet! When I recruited you to The Citadel I had hoped you'd become a star here. I even thought you would get elected team captain. Looks like both are at risk now!" As he put his arm on my shoulder pads, he said, "If you got to go to practice, no one will want to be around you, Vance. If you mope around and act like you don't want to be here, no one will really want to coach you, either. That's why this afternoon's practice will continue without you. You sit in the locker room alone until practice is over this morning. Then, go back to your room. If, after having time to think about what you really want, you decide you really want to play football, come back. Otherwise, I hope not to see you on this field again."

It was one of the loneliest mornings of my life.

That afternoon I was on the field 15 minutes before practice started. Coach Hall approached. I heard him say, "Where ya headin' this afternoon, Caesar?"

"I'm heading toward making you proud today, coach!" I said.

"Why do you want to do that?" he replied.

"Because I want to play football to make you proud, to make my dad proud, and I get to use the God-given talents I've been blessed with. Plus, who knows, maybe when I do really well, I'll even have more girlfriends," I chuckled.

"So, you *get* to practice today and not *got to* practice, like this morning?"

"Yes sir," I replied, as I turned to join the quarter-backs who were beginning to warm up their arms with lazy passes.

"Not yet, cadet!" he snapped. "Get back here." He grabbed my helmet and whispered into my ear, "You just learned the secret to having the kind of life you really want. Have more get to's than got to's!"

Meaningful Work:
How We Spend Our Time

Reds and Greens Story

Twelve years after that day at the football field, Van
about reds and greens while working with a gr
women recently diagnosed with breast cancer. He relates the
following story.

As we gathered around a table at the Key Largo resort
for a three-day retreat, Bill, the physician from Jackson
Memorial Medical Hospital with whom I was conduct-
ing the workshop, introduced me to the group. I asked
the women to please pull out their 10-day hourly log we
asked them to complete through noon today.

Bill handed each participant a green and a red highlighter, saying, "This weekend's not about cancer. It's
not about my being your oncologist. It's about reds and
greens. Please use your highlighters to mark each entry.
The red is for an entry that you remember representing
an hour that drained your energy. The green highlighter
is for an hour that energized you, enlightened you." The
desperate sadness was contagious as the red markers
began dominating each log.

When the women were done marking their logs, Bill
said, "Vance is here to help you manage reds and greens.
He is here this weekend to help you create at least 70 percent greens in your lives. As you do, you will become a
much more effective partner with me as I and your other
physicians help you manage your cancer and create more
of the life you want."

It was then that I began monitoring my life, too, noticing when I so often allowed the reds to outnumber the
greens. Since then, I have been using a red-green coach
to hold me accountable for making sure I have at least
90 percent greens in my life.

How would your log look? What will you do about
the reds? How will you maximize greens?

5

Energizing Relationships

Keep company with those who make you better.

—Unknown

The most important single ingredient in the formula of success is knowing how to get along with people.

—Theodore Roosevelt

A Relationship Story

Relationships that give you energy is key number four of Happy High Achievers.

"It's all about relationships," a Fortune 100 CEO once told Vance when he asked, "How do people get jobs like yours?"

When Vance was in his first year in college, he had a friend, Tim Slate. Tim invited Vance to come to his home for dinner. Vance accepted. At the designated time, a limousine sent by Mr. Slate picked up Vance and brought him to their home. Tim's father was the CEO of Fieldcrest Industries. They lived in New York in a fabulous home. It looked like a mansion to this 17-year-old freshman.

As Vance sat down to dinner at what seemed like a huge dining table, he wondered how anyone could have a job that could afford such a luxurious lifestyle. So he decided to ask Mr. Slate how he had managed to do so well.

"Mr. Slate, it looks like you have done really well in business. Could you share any tips with me that would help me?"

Mr. Slate looked intently at Vance, and replied, "Well, you see, it's all about who can trust you and who you can trust. It's about the stories others tell about you. Yes, it's all about relationships."

Vance thought about these words for a while. He was sure that something was missing. He decided to ask again.

"So, Mr. Slate, what would be your best advice to someone starting out on his career?"

Mr. Slate looked at Vance intently for a moment, and said, "It's about who can trust you and who you can trust. It's about the stories others tell about you. It's all about relationships."

The ability to form friendships, to make people believe in you and trust you, is one of the few absolutely fundamental qualities of success. Selling, buying, negotiating are so much smoother and easier when the parties enjoy each other's confidence. The young person who can make friends quickly will find that he/she will glide instead of stumbling through life.

—John J. McGuirk

It just didn't seem complete. As they were finishing dessert, Vance decided that he just had one more chance to find out the secret. He asked a third time for the secret to success.

This time Mr. Slate was pretty serious. He said, "Vance, if you were an employee of mine, I would have fired you by now for not hearing what I'm saying the first two times. Because you are a guest in our home, I'll answer your question again. The path to success is all about building relationships. It's about who trusts you and the stories people tell about you." He then excused himself from the table.

Needless to say, Vance did not make a positive impression on Mr. Slate. But Mr. Slate's advice made an indelible impression on Vance! Over 40 years later, the advice from this experience still rings true.

What relationships are you building?

"Getting" More Than We're "Giving" in *Each* Relationship

If you'll forget the things you give
And ne'er forget what you receive;
Quite soon you'll make a host of friends
Who'll gladly aid you to achieve.

—Alonzo Newton Benn

Now here is the counterintuitive part. Happy High Achievers have relationships that "get" them more than they "give." How? By giving to the relationship with love and a sense of gratitude, not a sense of scorekeeping or expectations of payback.

We all give to another in a relationship. When we give because it feels good or right to us, we "get." An example is one spouse who "gives" the other a prestigious house or tuition for school. It feels good to do that. When one gives because it's what the other person values most (time together, validation, or a wonderful memory together), then this giving with love and gratitude pays even larger dividends to the giver. It sounds like a paradox, getting through giving.

Who is responsible for each partner—in any relationship—getting more than he or she gives? Both! And when that is happening, both are attracted to the relationship, and there is no room for resentment. On the other hand, if one thinks he or she is giving more than getting, it's easy for that seed of resentment to sprout into a huge tree, creating a cycle broken only with intervention that's often painful and expensive.

Relationships are central to getting what we want in life. Therefore, creating relationships that give us energy is crucial to being a Happy High Achiever. These include our personal and professional relationships and those who mentor and coach us.

Every man, however wise, needs the advice of some sagacious friend in the affairs of life.

—Plautus

The Story of the Geese

We first heard about the geese many years ago at a meeting, and then saw the story again recently in a circulating e-mail. In neither case was there an author. We share it with you, wishing we knew the person who thought of it.

Have you ever noticed geese flying in a V formation? Science has discovered some interesting information about the results of the geese flying in this way.

As each bird flaps its wings, it creates an advantage for the bird immediately following. With the V formation, this uplift advantage increases the flock's flying range by at least 70 percent!

The geese take turns being the leader. When the head goose gets tired, it returns to the formation and another goose takes up the point position.

If a goose decides to fall out of the formation, it experiences the drag and resistance of going it alone. That goose then quickly gets back into the formation to be able to utilize the lifting power of the goose in front.

If you have ever watched geese fly overhead, you probably also heard a lot of honking. The geese honk from behind to encourage those in the front to keep up their speed.

When a goose falls out of the formation because it is sick or hurt, two other geese will follow it down to offer protection and help. They stay with the fallen goose until it dies or is able to resume flying. Only then will the geese resume flying.

Geese know how to create relationships that give them energy!

What Can We Learn From Geese?

- Certainly geese teach the importance of hanging out with those who give them energy.
- Those who share a common purpose and vision can get to where they are going faster and with less energy.
- Sharing the responsibility of demanding jobs allows all to benefit.
- Sharing encouraging words that fit the situation propels all to keep moving toward the destination.
- Caring about one another gives each individual the best chance to achieve his or her goals.
- Happy High Achievers are a lot like geese. They look for ways to add energy to their own and others' lives.
- They work on increasing their self-awareness to detect when they are draining others.
- They take responsibility for selecting relationships that add to their energy.

A friendship founded on business is a good deal better than a business founded on friendship.

—John D. Rockefeller

Relationships With Stakeholders

Interdependent

Independent

Dependent

The making of friends who are real friends is the best token we have of a person's success in life.

—Edward E. Hale

No one's happiness but my own is in my power to achieve or to destroy.

—Ayn Rand

Happy High Achievers have key relationships that give them energy, especially with "stakeholders."

Stakeholders are those people who have interest in and influence over your success or failure to be the Happy High Achiever you aspire to be. Spouses, partners, bosses, key clients, children, and bosses' assistants can be some of your top stakeholders. The management of stakeholder relationships is central to Happy High Achieving, so much so that we've seen many Happy High Achievers periodically rate their relationships with stakeholders. An example of a Stakeholder Relationship Scoreboard is in the Resource section at the end of this book.

Successful relationship management also includes knowing when you are in a dependent relationship. One clue is the pronouns and nouns you hear yourself use. They, she, he, headquarters, the office, and the management are the terms of dependence. Independence, on the other hand, is described by pronouns such as I, me, and mine. This is a healthy developmental phase normally seen in teens as the person individuates, or creates identity or individuality. This is an important stage prior to interdependence.

Interdependence is the foundation for relationships without resentment, where both "get" more than they "give." Pronouns of interdependence are "we," "us," and "our." Interdependence recognizes the involvement that we have in others' lives and they in ours. This is true in our families, at work, and with friends.

Happy High Achievers know the difference between interdependence and dependence on the other's dependence. They focus on interdependence, especially in their core relationships.

Happy High Achievers realize the sobering truth that we are accountable to ourselves for our current relationships!

Making Time for Relationships

- Get all the balls into the treasure chest.

- Big balls include family, friends, career relationships, personal growth, spiritual path.

- Prioritize who and what is most important to you to include in your life.

- Unless you place the big balls in first, they won't fit later. If you first fill your life with the unimportant or small things, there is no time, energy, or other resources for the important.

- Only after the most important people and things are put onto your calendar are other items added.

- What do you put into your treasure chest first, second, and third?

In 1973, we were privileged to hear Alvah H. Chapman, Jr.—at that time CEO of Knight Newspapers—tell a story about priorities. The following is a paraphrasing of that enlightening story.

Imagine that you have been given an extraordinary treasure chest. It could be made of intricately carved wood, gleaming metals, jewels, or any material you can imagine.

The chest is quite large. It's larger than you would normally think a treasure chest to be. As you approach the chest, you notice that the lid is closed. There is no latch locking the chest. You can open the lid by merely reaching out and lifting it.

Upon lifting the lid you peer into the treasure chest and see that it is empty! You very quickly notice that off to the side of the chest are many different balls of different sizes, a pile of sand, and a container of water.

As you gaze at these materials, there is a wise mentor who explains the situation. All the various materials represent the various areas comprising your life. Your task is to place all the materials into your life treasure chest.

The task is overwhelming, you say. You lament that there is far more outside the chest than can be put into the chest! What will you leave out?

Your wise guide instructs you to place the largest balls into the chest first. In the spaces in between go the smaller balls. Once this is accomplished, the sand is then poured into the spaces between the smallest balls. At the very last, the water is poured into the spaces between the grains of sand.

What Do Most People Want in Their Relationships?

To be listened to = **L**

To be understood = **U**

To be validated = **V**

Empathy = **E**

When people feel listened to, understood, and validated, they get empathy and they feel "LUVE." This is a way of showing empathy.

If you're here to contribute love, you'll die happy. If you're here to get loved, you'll die disappointed.

Unknown

It has consistently been our observation and experience that most people are trying to be understood by others. Notice for yourself. Go through just one day observing other people's behavior.

We have made up a process to help give understanding and empathy to others. When we are with someone, we do our best to *really* hear what the person is saying and to give some kind of tangible feedback that we understood what he or she was saying or trying to say.

When a person is speaking, we first give tangible evidence that we are listening by looking at him or her. That does not include glancing at the computer screen, TV, or newspaper, or being distracted by our own thoughts. It does mean being attentive to the person's words and feelings. It does not mean trying to fix anything. We just listen and observe.

Then, inside our own heads, we consider what the person seems to be trying to say and what words express his or her feelings. This is the understand portion. It is important to note that we are the only persons in the exchange who know this process is going on. Until we do or say something tangible, the speaker does not know we are trying to understand. We do our best to understand.

At appropriate times, we actually say to the speaker what we think the essence is of what he or she is saying, and how the person is possibly feeling. We might only nod our head or have a facial expression that is a tangible sign that we are listening and understanding. This is validation.

This is our formula for showing empathy. It's a tangible manifestation to the speaker that he or she is important enough to be listened to, understood, and validated. Give it a try sometime. Even if it's not done well at first, there is usually credit given for the attempt. Anything worth doing is worth doing poorly at first.

6

Beliefs and Behaviors That Give You Peace

Most people are about as happy as they make up their minds to be.

—Abraham Lincoln

Beliefs and Behaviors ⇒ Peace

- A way to replace chaos with quiet

- Spiritual oneness with all

- Emotional centeredness

- A way to be safe . . . without fear

- Reframing events

Happiness is only a by-product of successful living.

—Dr. Austen Fox Riggs

Beliefs and behaviors that create peace is key number five held by Happy High Achievers. While there are many "standard" ways of creating peace, the options are almost limitless.

HHAs adopt a system of practices that replace chaos with peace. Prayer, meditation, running, wilderness hiking, the athlete's "zone," skiing with a gentle mind, and spending time each day to think about a real positive in your life and to express gratitude for it are frequent peacemaking behaviors of Happy High Achievers. Changing beliefs to be more comfortable saying "No" to some requests would allow for more peace for some. For others, it might be learning to be more organized.

One HHA we know uses the time spent at traffic lights to take deep breaths that increase peace in his life. "I love three lights," he used to tell his friends. Of course, he was referring to three very deep breaths he would take as the traffic signal was going from yellow to red back to green.

Another useful tool is the Serenity Prayer. It encourages one to figure out what one has control over and what one does not.

God grant me the serenity to accept the things I cannot control,

The courage to change the things I can,

And the wisdom to know the difference.

Stephen Covey describes something similar. He refers to the area of concern and the area of influence: the more the two overlap, the less the stress.

Decrease Stress, Increase Peace

- Change perceptions and interpretations.

- Overcome stressful life events.

- Understand that stress is a belief that you cannot cope with the situation.

- Determine your own responses to stressors.

We sow our thoughts, and we reap our actions;
We sow our actions, and we reap our habits;
We sow our habits, and we reap our characters;
We sow our characters, and we reap our destiny.

—Charles Hall

Stress is usually a function of our own thinking, which is influenced by our beliefs. That is, we interpret something as stressful or not, except for the most extreme conditions. Stress and its opposite, peace, are usually subjective experiences.

Vance tells a story about how he learned to respond to stressors. "As I cleared the first hurdle in the Florida State High School Championships in 1962, I felt a slap against my right shoulder. The adjacent runner had been coached to 'knock' me off my race by hitting my shoulder before I got out front. It worked. I glanced at him with surprise and anger before I regained what had become habitually a peacefully powerful stride that had propelled me to never lose a high school hurdles race."

Vance won this race, setting a record that stood for 23 years. Pappy Holt, his hurdles coach, met him at the finish line. Holt, who had volunteered to work with high school athletes during 1961 and 1962, was one of Vance's most influential life coaches. He knew how to be world class. He had just returned from coaching the American Olympic hurdlers the previous two years.

Coach Holt rhetorically asked, "Did you see what you did? You gave away part of your race by paying attention to the runner who hit you!

"You see, Vance, in life, you're going to get hit. What you do in response will define your life more than anything you do. Choose your race, see it, feel it, and run it peacefully without paying attention to your detractors. That's how to be world class in whatever you do."

Stress and managing stress are mainly in the eye of the beholder. Start to notice when you feel stressed and begin to utilize some options that help you to view the event differently or to manage it differently.

Many of you have seen and taken a questionnaire that lists 30–40 events thought to be stressful. Each event experienced during the last year is dutifully checked off. Each event is given a number of points from 10–100 to rate the stressfulness of that event. The number of points for one's stressful events is then added up. Having more than 300 points was considered to be a precursor to some illness occurring.

It was noted in research in the 1960s and 1970s that about 80 percent of people scoring more than 300 points did have some illness. Then, in the late 1970s, Suzanne Kobasa studied the 20 percent who did not become ill, and labeled them hardy personalities. These people had ways of negotiating what had been described as stressful life events. They had ways of overcoming adversity.

Consider the following diagram as a definition of stress:

Event $\Rightarrow$ Appraisal of the situation and our ability to handle it $\Rightarrow$ Believe we can cope $\Rightarrow$ Act

Event $\Rightarrow$ Appraisal of the situation and our ability to handle it $\Rightarrow$ Believe we cannot cope = Stress

An event happens. It could be something that has actually occurred or something only in our thinking. It can be just about anything.

We then go through a very quick appraisal determining if we can or cannot handle the stressor, and what we could do to handle it and what could happen if we do not. This appraisal process is influenced by our beliefs about ourselves and our world view. We'll talk about beliefs in the next section.

When we come to the conclusion that we can cope with the event, then we act and handle the event.

When we come to the conclusion that we cannot cope with the event, then we have stress. Stress is generally a fear or concern about not being able to handle something or having to pay too big a price to manage the event.

The world we have created is a product of our thinking. It cannot be changed without changing our thinking.

—Albert Einstein

Being Aware of Your Beliefs

- Beliefs impact our lives.

- We may not be aware of beliefs.

- Beliefs can be modified.

This is a good time to give some attention to becoming more aware of your beliefs. In our retreats for leaders, executives, principals, boards, and graduate students, we offer an opportunity for participants to become more conscious of their beliefs.

Since these beliefs have such an impact on our lives, we encourage each of you to take some time to really think about the next exercise. You might walk away from the exercise for a while to give it more thought. You might start writing whatever comes into your mind. You can always go back and revise.

There are many more than four areas of beliefs. We have chosen the following four because these topics surface so often in our work with clients.

On four different pages, list your top 10 beliefs (the ones most important to you) about each of the following four areas.

- *Loves* = Things, people, experiences, and dreams you love that give you ease or peace;

- *Fears* = Things, people, experiences, and dreams you fear, that give you distress or dis-ease;

- *Gifts* = Your unique life experiences, talents, interests, skills, or strengths;

- *Truths* = The "if, thens" in your life. Examples include "If I am happy, then I will be healthier," "If I can find something about you I can love, then I will have no fear of you," "If I trust you, then I will get hurt."

  Truths also include the core statements in our life. Examples include "My world is full of opportunity" and "My world is pretty scary."

Loves

1. _____

2. _____

3. _____

4. _____

5. _____

6. _____

7. _____

8. _____

9. _____

10. _____

Fears

1. _____

2. _____

3. _____

4. _____

5. _____

6. _____

7. _____

8. _____

9. _____

10. _____

Gifts

1. _____

2. _____

3. _____

4. _____

5. _____

6. _____

7. _____

8. _____

9. _____

10. _____

Truths

1. _____

2. _____

3. _____

4. _____

5. _____

6. _____

7. _____

8. _____

9. _____

10. _____

Now highlight in green those that give you love or peace. Highlight in red those that give you fear or distress. How much more emphasis could you give the greens? Which red ones have become obsolete in your life today? Which red ones could you give less emphasis to, or even change to greens?

Increasing Peace and Happiness

Make a Decision to Be Happy

Finally, brethren, whatever things are true, whatever things are honest, whatever things are just, whatever things are pure, whatever things are of good report; if there be any virtue, and if there be any praise, think on these things.

—Paul, to the Philippians

In 1999, Carol Ann decided she wanted to build a new house on the lot where we currently were living. The following is her story about maintaining a happy attitude during one of life's more notorious stressors.

I had a general floor plan in mind, which I took to several architects. Finally, one was chosen. We began a process of fine-tuning many details. A designer came in to add ideas of a more aesthetic nature.

The original plans were changed to scale down square footage and cost. Eventually, applications were made to the city and the coastal commission. After about two years, all the permits were obtained. Then a process of selecting a contractor and working out a contract began. Eventually, the old house was demolished, and the new one begun. It is now mid-2005. We are almost ready to move in.

I've intentionally not listed all the setbacks and demands of this project, because that is not the point. The point is that no matter what happened or how long something took, I had made up my mind from the beginning that I was going to be happy doing this project. Events could be viewed with frustration, or as exciting challenges to be overcome.

This way of experiencing each day is what has helped the Pike Fish Company become the success it is today. The people working there have a video, which relates that each person decides how he or she is going to feel that day at work. Like them, we choose every day to be happy, sad, frustrated, or excited.

More Practices

- **Living in the moment**

- **Acceptance of the moment**

- **Focused breathing**

- **Self-talk**

So often, we all "live" in a place that does not exist in reality. This would be a time that has already passed or a time that has not happened. While "living" in these places in our heads, it seems pretty real and even creates physiological responses to what is being thought!

A practice of creating peace in the moment is called "mindfulness." The key is to notice what we are thinking and feeling and to notice what is actually happening at the moment. This actually empowers us to deal with what is really going on, rather than being disempowered trying to get a handle on something that doesn't exist.

It is difficult to feel peace while trying to create and manage in the moment something that does not exist in that very moment. Much of our unhappiness comes from not being willing to accept the reality of what has happened. This is a form of denial. It takes a lot of energy to keep it going!

One of the easiest ways to quickly generate a feeling of peace is to use your own breathing process. It's done in seconds. Just focus on your breath. Notice the physical sensations of the breath in. Then breathe out a long, relaxing exhalation, again noticing how that feels.

One of the advantages to the focused breathing is that it gives your brain a break from your thoughts and the self-talk going on in your head. If this talk is critical and negative, it often leaves you feeling a lack of peace and comfort. Begin to notice how you talk to yourself. If we followed you around and talked to you the way you talk to you, would you want us to stay around?

For Whom Are You Living Your Life?

- **Is it for yourself ? Is that selfish?**

- **Is it for others? Who then sets the priorities?**

In our various groups we coach, we like to ask the question, "For whom are you living your life?" Most start out by listing a number of people including spouses, bosses, children, God, friends, charitable organizations, etc. Imagine being pulled in so many directions by competing forces.

In our experience, when people live their lives for themselves, based on what they have determined to be their purpose, they decide on their priorities. They are grounded in what is right for them rather than being stretched to meet others' priorities. Deciding on one's own priorities can increase a sense of being grounded and peaceful. Paradoxically, the people we work with using the Happy High Achiever model are also contributors to the people and causes that are important to them.

Consider that what you decide you love to do to serve others (your purpose) gives you more than what you give. Many ancient teachings subscribe to this way of attaining peace and happiness.

Buddha, Muhammad, Jesus, and Moses are all attributed with statements that teach their followers to think about what they want from others and to give that away. This is the way to a better life. Their teachings include statements like the following: See yourself in others. Then whom can you hurt? There is a reward for your treatment of every living thing. Love thy neighbor as thou lovest thyself. Do unto others as you would have them do unto you.

So as we decide what is the way we want to be in service to others—because that is our gift and our calling and we give that—then we create peace, contentment, and more happiness.

More Beliefs
That Lead to Peace

- Letting go of resentment

- Forgiving others

- Forgiving oneself

Hanging on to resentment hinders finding peace for yourself. It also allows the transgressor to control you and your responses. The opposite of this is forgiveness.

Forgiveness does not have to be done for the transgressor. It's done for yourself! If not, then the damage and hurt continue. There is a saying from 12-step programs about this. You are allowing someone to rent space in your head for free. You're stuck and not able to move on while you live in the past.

Forgiveness is something that most of us don't want to do when we feel we have been wronged. We're afraid it will send the wrong message to the offender. What most of us don't realize is that we don't have to tell the other person. We can just let it go and move on with our own choices of how we want to think and feel.

One of the more difficult things for so many to do is to forgive themselves. This is especially true of people with low self-esteem.

This is a good time to review The Quiz from the section on responsibility in the Introduction. This may be especially helpful if it still seems not to be true. Accepting it as true is one way we create peace for ourselves. If you have always done the most important thing for you to do at that time, given the information you had at that time, wouldn't it be easier to forgive yourself and others?

7

Three R's

Review, Renew, Recommit

*The wise will always reflect on the quality,
not the quantity of life.*

—Seneca

Three R's

Review, Renew, and Recommit

- **The cycle of rebirth or re-creation within our lives and businesses**

- **A process of creating clarity within ourselves**

- **Reflection that is committed to taking advantage of expanding possibilities**

- **Setting aside time to rearrange priorities and endless possibilities of purpose, vision, work, play, relationships, health, and spirituality**

The important thing is not to stop questioning.

—Albert Einstein

The three R's round out the first six of our seven keys. This happens when you review, renew your focus, and recommit to it, updating your purpose, vision, work, play, relationships, health, and spirituality.

In pursuing the three R's, we are like a tree committed to growing by renewing where it is, relative to its energy source (the sun), recommitting on a direction that stays in line with the life-supporting energy of the sun. As soon as the tree decides to stop adjusting its attention to the sun's new angle, it has decided to die. We're the same.

Other important people in our lives can be a part of this process. If possible, share this with the really important people in your life. Encourage them to share with you. You can be each other's accountability partner and cheering team. Success increases as we enlist supportive others.

Coaches, teachers, and mentors can play a vital role in this process. They can help us assess our lives based on our purpose, vision, work, relationships, beliefs, and behaviors.

One way to do the three R's is to set aside a day or even a week each year away from all the "to-do's." It is a time to say good-bye to what is too comfortable and outdated. It is a time to say hello to meaningful change that will result in meaningful happiness.

This is a time for asking ourselves questions that will

- Hold ourselves accountable for designing our lives;
- Assess how we are living our goals;
- Refine our long-term purpose and vision;
- Define short-term goals to achieve purpose and vision;
- Review what worked, what did not;
- Create a design and plan for the future;
- Reflect on all facets of our lives to find clarity and balance.

Retreats

We could have put retreats in the Beliefs and Behaviors chapter. Retreats can be used for both.

Retreats can be as short as a few seconds to as long as a sabbatical of, say, a year.

Shorter retreats are usually the ones we take in our minds. They include breathing techniques, short exercises easily accomplished while taking a mini-break from some other activity, and some that you can make up for yourself. There are many books on relaxation techniques that offer other ideas. One of the best of these is *The Relaxation and Stress Reduction Workbook* by Davis, Eshelman, and McKay.

Longer retreats usually take a little more planning. They are times we set aside to be away from our normal routines and responsibilities. Sometimes they are planned alone, and sometimes we include others.

They may be self-programmed or designed by professionals. One of the best known of these is Canyon Ranch. They offer many options at their various locations.

We know of leaders who schedule one week every quarter as a Think Week. This is a time to think about the bigger picture, which includes considering global conditions and other big subjects. This is a way to put what they are doing the other 12 weeks of the quarter into perspective. While many of us would not put that much time into considering such a large view, it certainly is a guide to referencing what we are doing to a larger perspective of our surroundings. We support that 60,000-foot look down on your life periodically to explore what patterns are working well and what patterns could work better in a more global, universal context.

We suggest that you consider your resources of time and money when deciding on what works best for you and your situation. When these resources are limited, most people can find a half day every quarter to review where they have been and where they are going.

In our American culture, there are two times of year associated with new beginnings. These two times are in September and in January. September is when we went back to school with all the potential of the new school year. January is associated with New Year's resolutions. The three R's are so much more than that. They include discovering what ignites us so that we will want to engage. They also include plans and preparations that move us toward accomplishment.

In *The Paradox of Success,* John O'Neil offers many ideas about retreats, which could be helpful in planning yours.

Search for a single, inclusive good is doomed to failure. Such happiness as life is capable of comes from the full participation of all our powers in the endeavor to wrest from each changing situation of experience its own full and unique meaning.

—John Dewey

Now and Then
Résumé or Picture

Write a résumé for now based on the job and experiences that you now have.

Next, write a résumé for three years from now based on the job you see yourself having. Identify the accomplishments you will have on your future résumé.

Rank these accomplishments in the order of their importance.

Comparing your future résumé to your current one gives you a road map of what projects to take on or not. The idea is to create the work you want for yourself that is aligned with the life you want.

Another similar activity is a visual one. Draw a picture of yourself now, your life now, you in your life now.

Next, draw a picture of the life you want to create in the next three years. Use crayons, markers, sparkles, or other embellishments that help capture your ideal life. Two coaches we know, Karen McBride and Beverly Stacey, offer workshops to help people create their ideal futures by using pictures from magazines. This helps stimulate ideas and creativity.

The following is only a short list of questions you can ask about your picture and achieving it:

- Who and what do you include in your picture?
- Who and what do you leave out?
- Is there meaningful work?
- Does your picture feel light, serious, heavy, bright?
- Does that match what you want?
- What would it take to get to the ideal?
- What are beginning steps you could take?
- Whom could you enlist as supporters?
- What financial matters need to be addressed?
- Do you want more school or training?

The moment we definitely commit ourselves, providence moves, too. Whatever you can do or dream you can, begin it. Boldness has genius, power, and magic in it.

—Goethe

Now Résumé

Then Résumé

Your Life Picture Now

Your Life Picture Then

Most Important
Thing to Control

One of the questions we ask people is, "What is the most important thing for you to control?" When people have been living their lives so that the most important things for them to control are

- Other people's perceptions;
- Other people's behaviors;
- Other people's experience; and
- Other people's feelings;

they usually become exhausted.

We notice that when people live their lives so that the most important things to control are

- Their own perceptions;
- Their own behaviors;
- Their own experience; and
- Their own feelings;

they have a shortcut to creating fulfillment and happiness. In short, these people are not trying to control that which they cannot control.

So, what would you say is the most important thing for you to control? It might be your time, maybe it is the people you think can hurt you, maybe it is others' behavior, the grades your students earn, or your principal's or boss's perceptions. While some of these things are probably important to you, it can be helpful and empowering to remember that you have the control over your own engagement and behaviors and choices.

These become focused and meaningful when determined in the context of your purpose while keeping your vision in front of you.

We both like a little book by Ruiz, *The Four Agreements*. It is a poignant reminder to always do your best and to keep your word. These are our own proactive behaviors over which we have control.

Verbal Business Card

The Verbal Business Card (VBC) is the answer we give people when they ask us what we do. It is one of the most frequently asked questions in a social setting. It is really helpful to have a well-thought-out answer that creates the brand, the position, the reputation that you want. Of course, deciding what you want all of those to be can be the difficult part. That is why it is helpful to consider developing your VBC during your RRR time.

What we notice about Happy High Achievers is that they have a brand that is aligned with their purpose and vision. Having this alignment, they are able to tell people what they do quickly and succinctly while they have the other person's attention. That attention rarely lasts more than about 30 seconds.

VBC answers the questions of whom do you serve, and in what unique way do you serve that person. So be distinctive, with a very authentic answer that often is the first impression others will remember about you.

Your Verbal Business Card

360 Review

Three-sixties are a way to get feedback from others. This feedback, when done constructively, can be useful during the three R's process.

There are all kinds of off-the-shelf 360 assessments. We use one by Kouzes and Posner called Leadership Practices Inventory (LPI). Three-sixties can also be created using customized competencies.

Here are steps for creating your own customized, competency-based 360. Think about your current job, personal situation, or whatever area of your life on which you would like feedback. If it is your job, what are the five most important competencies you would look for in a person who would succeed you?

Once you have identified these five, then you rank yourself on these competencies. Use a score of 0 to 10 to describe where you believe you rank. Then you would select others you trust to be supportive, trustworthy, and honest to also rank you. These might include peers, principals, bosses, direct reports, or others whose input you value. Sometimes these scores are given without the rater's name, and sometimes it is done with their identification.

A spin on this technique is for you to rank the five competencies in order of their importance. How are you doing on number one?

Another spin is to have your supervisor, principal, manager, or boss rank the five in importance to them. Just knowing their priorities can be helpful to you in setting goals and deciding which action items to put into an already busy schedule.

We frequently use a narrative, generic type of 360. We usually have three questions that we ask the chosen responders to answer. When we get all the answers, we put the answers for each question together, and do not identify who gave each answer.

The questions we use are

1. What are two or three items that are done well or creating positive results?

2. What are one or two things that could be better?

3. If you had a magic wand, what is one thing you would do to help this person be even more successful?

The general idea is to decide what is important to you and to people important to you, and to get a measure of how you and they think you are doing. Is there alignment in your and their ratings? If not, what could be done to create better unity? What are action items that can be taken to improve your scores if you repeat this process?

In our experience, it is important to follow up 360s with a plan and action. When this is not done, the respondents often feel that it was a waste of their time to be involved.

Three R's Questions
and Behaviors

The following are questions, behaviors, and suggestions from which you can choose to address in your retreat times. Hopefully, they will also help generate your creativity of questions that are important to you.

Schedule seven hours per year away from all "to-do's" as you review, renew, and recommit to what you want in your relationships, career, and general life growth.

Determine the various roles you have in your full life, and goals for each around which your time is managed.

What are milestones during the last year, month, day, and moment to be celebrated? How would you meaningfully celebrate?

What is most important to you? Second? Third?

What are the most important parts of your life? How do you demonstrate their importance? What would allow you to spend more time on these?

Where or on what do you actually spend most of your time?

Use Covey's two-by-two matrix of what is important and non-urgent (See *The 7 Habits of Highly Successful People*).

Do your time and importance lists match? If not, where would you like to make some small, beginning changes to spend time on what is most important?

What current goals are in alignment with your purpose and vision?

Which current goals are not in alignment with your purpose and vision? How might you address these?

What are new goals for the next quarter? Year? Life?

What are small steps toward a fantastic goal?

What financials need to be in order to achieve goals?

How are you taking care of yourself

- Physically?
- Educationally?
- Emotionally?
- Spiritually?

Do you want to set aside time for any of the above four?

Get a thorough health exam by a qualified professional. Use the results to outline your path to a healthier, more energized you. Remember, it is often the small things done regularly that add up to big results.

With the information from your health exam, set up goals that will help you to have more energy and to be healthier.

Evaluate any educational needs required to meet your goals. What would it take to meet these? What are the first steps in accomplishing these?

Plan a trip around your spiritual growth. Go on that trip!

What do you enjoy? What brings you pleasure?

Does your living space feel right and support your goals?

Look over the journal you have been keeping to learn more about what really interested you, the reds and the greens.

Contract with yourself to notice what you are doing in the moment and to notice the feelings, the skills, and the strengths you have.

What is missing?

Ask yourself what you have considered in the past that would be important to include in your life (or at least to investigate).

What relationships do you want to deepen? Explore? Let go of?

For what and by whom do you want to be remembered? Are you engaging in behaviors that will get you that remembrance?

Write what you want your eulogy to be. Who would you like to deliver it, and what would you like for them to say about you? How can you start working today to achieve the results you want?

Are your behaviors in alliance with your values and ethics? If not, what obstacles need to be overcome?

What is a good question you could be asking yourself?

What is a good question your partner could ask you?

Participate in periodic workshops with similar-minded people.

Challenge your assumptions. What are your 10 truths? Is there any other way to consider these? Are they always true?

Select three to five major priorities that are in alignment with your purpose. Write down steps to accomplish these, along with finish dates.

Use the Happy High Achiever Scorecard (see Resource) to help indicate where you have made progress and in what areas you wish to emphasize changes.

Will you include the important, supportive people in your life in this process?

Anything worth doing is worth doing poorly at first.

—Anonymous

8

Discipline

First say to yourself what you would be; then do what you have to do.

—Epictetus

Discipline

- **A system, infrastructure, habit, or core value that gives us the freedom to get into shape and to stay in the shape we really want**

- **A way of living each day**

- **The strength to say no**

- **The courage to say yes**

Someone has well said, "Success is a journey, not a destination." Happiness is to be found along the way, not at the end of the road.

—Robert R. Updegraff

Now the bad news!

Getting into happy high achieving shape and staying there takes discipline. Self-regulation has consistently been mentioned over thousands of years as a key to happiness. In Dhammapada, Buddha says, "By . . . self-control and self mastery the wise one may make an island that a flood cannot sweep away."

In his mega-bestseller, *The Road Less Traveled*, Scott Peck writes, "Without discipline we can solve nothing. With only some discipline we can solve only some problems. With total discipline we can solve all problems." He also points out that a person who has the ability to delay gratification has the key to psychological maturity and fulfillment.

Creating and adapting a system, infrastructure, habit, or "values" that gives us the freedom to get into shape and stay there is hard work, in part because it involves saying no. Saying no is one of the things high achievers avoid at almost all costs. Happy High Achievers have the strength to say no to that which interferes with their living their purpose and vision.

On the other hand, it takes courage to say yes to that to which we are drawn, to declare it, and to set in motion what it takes to achieve the fullest potential of our purpose. The discipline involved in this pursuit makes a significant difference in our lives, which is then the gift we give to others.

The following story is an example of learning about having the discipline to say no.

Backpack Story

Discipline does not always mean to say yes and take on more. Sometimes, it takes discipline to do less. Vance tells the following story of how he learned when to say no to something.

When I was 32, my coach, Byron Harless, recommended I go to Outward Bound. OB is a wilderness training program with lessons for the rest of one's life. After flying to North Carolina and meeting my group and our leaders, we began to make plans for a five-day hike.

The first hour culminated in the 10 of us having our personal gear from our backpacks all laid out in a circle. Then inside the circle was a pile of group gear. There were ropes, fuel bottles, cooking pans and utensils, first aid supplies, food, and tarps.

We first lightened our loads by eliminating redundant personal gear. The second thing we did was divvy up the group necessities. I thought that what I should do was to take much more than my fair share of the group load. I took a little more than half of the weight of the group gear by taking two large climbing ropes, which I put on my shoulders, and two fuel bottles. I was proud of myself for carrying so much of the load.

We started out on our five-day hike in the Linville Wilderness Area, going over hilly terrain to get from one mountain to another. By the end of the day, I had positioned myself in front of the group, going to lookout points to help us stay on course.

We slept the first night. I knew I was tired. On the second day, I continued to be the one who used more energy than anyone else. I continued carrying more weight than others and going out front.

By 3:00 p.m. on the second day, I collapsed from sheer exhaustion.

Two women and a man in the group came to my aid. They took the ropes off my shoulders, helped me remove my backpack, and gave me water. I felt very humbled. The group had to stop earlier than planned to accommodate my collapse.

Hot soup was prepared and brought to me. As I sipped the soup, I thought, "I'll bet they really appreciate how hard I worked for the group."

As I finished the soup, one of the instructors asked the group to huddle around me. He asked them a question, "How do you feel about Vance?"

As I was waiting to hear how much they appreciated all my extra efforts, the first person spoke up. "I have resented him from the moment he gobbled up so much of the load. I felt he disrespected all of us and our ability to carry our fair load. Now that he has exhausted himself and slowed us down, I want him out of our group." The comments did not get any better as each person spoke similarly.

I thought about how this relates back to my work. Often there are people like myself who carry much more than their fair share who seem to want to control. People around them grow resentful, fold their arms, and feel disrespected by the ones who are kidding themselves thinking that they are heroes, that they should be thanked, and that they are now entitled to more.

Vance learned that the respectful thing for him to do is to allow each person to carry his or her fair amount. It's OK for people to take on responsibility so they too can grow, become stronger, and more fulfilled.

Characteristics of Discipline

- **Perseverance**

- **Willpower**

- **Desire**

- **Drive**

- **Purpose**

- **Goals**

- **Accountability**

A journey of a thousand miles begins with one step.

—Chinese proverb

A Stanford psychologist began what became a well-known study in 1921. Genius-level children were followed throughout their lifetimes. One of the study's findings was that those who attained high levels of accomplishment had the characteristics of perseverance, willpower, and desire. All of these help to define our use of the word "discipline."

Happy High Achievers use their drive, purpose, and discipline to become inwardly pleased with themselves (high self-esteem), while still pushing forward to make a difference in ways that are individually and collectively important.

In *Flow,* Mihaly Csikszentmihalyi studied the "waste of free time." Paradoxically, people long to leave their jobs and enjoy their free time while actually having more opportunity at work to engage in flow activities with goals, feedback, and challenges. He states, "Hobbies that demand skill, habits that set goals and limits, personal interests, and especially inner discipline help to make leisure what it is supposed to be—a chance for re-creation." In an interview for the American Psychological Association's *Monitor,* Csikszentmihalyi asked, "If we are so rich, why aren't we happy?" He answers with, "Research shows that active involvement in one's work, family, and community are the ways in which people end up having a good life."

In *Priorities* magazine, we read an article about Oprah. In it is the statement, "her commitment to discipline stands out." Examples of that discipline are how she chose and followed through on creating a consistent routine to create better health for herself. It sets an example for others and shows her living her own ideal of being responsible for her life. Captain Eddie Rickenbacker, a pioneer in the aviation industry, reflected a similar attitude with his remark, "I can give you a six-word formula for success: Think things through—then follow through."

Victims of Change

What they do:

- Ignore it

- Avoid it

- Become assively aggressive

- Become overtly aggressive, revolt/retreat (leave)

If we continually try to force a child to do what he is afraid to do, he will become more timid and will use his brains and energy, not to explore the unknown, but to find ways to avoid the pressures we put on him.

—John Holt

Happy High Achievers lead or initiate change that allows them to have the discipline they need to continue achieving. They are not victims of change who ignore it, avoid it, or get passively aggressive or even resentful when it's occurring.

James Allen mentions in *As a Man Thinketh*, "Most of us are anxious to improve our circumstances, but are unwilling to improve ourselves—and we therefore remain bound."

Happiness and fulfillment do not happen when the old self is stuck in its old way. We want to cling to old familiar behaviors because they have become comfortable and easy, even when they are not in our best interests.

Unhappy high achievers are nearly always unconscious of their own lack of fulfillment until faced with "open space" of job loss, mortality, or the loss of a loved one. It is then, in the calm of the eye of the hurricane, that they often consider change, which then requires discipline.

Knowing that we are the engineers of our own change leaves us with accepting our own responsibility for creating the lives we want. We take responsibility for the way we respond to others' demands for our change. We let go of blaming others. This freedom can be both daunting and motivating.

Examples of Discipline Used by Happy High Achievers

- A routine or habit experienced as part of who we are, around which we live

- Accountability groups

- Journal writing

- Yearly goal setting with quarterly markers

- Delaying gratification while celebrating milestones

- A coach and a coaching process that keep you focused

One of the greatest talents of all is the talent to recognize and to develop talent in others.

—Frank Tyger

There has been much written about emotional intelligence (EI). One of the tenets of EI, according to the work of Daniel Goleman, is the importance of personal motivation, practice, and feedback on one's ability to increase EI and be able to reach one's goals. This sounds like the essence of discipline.

Techniques for our personal management include the list to the left. We strongly believe in including mentors, coaches, and educators in our process of developing discipline to act in the ways we most desire. They can be instrumental in asking the right questions and offering ideas for us to achieve creative responses to setbacks and obstacles.

One of our mutual role models for developing discipline is George Leonard. In his book, *Mastery*, he shares one of the most important concepts to developing discipline. He tells us that the path of the master's journey is the opposite of the quick fix. It is learning to enjoy the plateaus that come when learning a new endeavor. These are the times when there is practice with no appearance of change or growth. The person who would master continues to practice and practice until reaching the next observable progress.

Leonard teaches, "If our life is a good one, a life of mastery, most of it will be spent on the plateau. If not, a large part of it may well be spent in restless, distracted, ultimately self-destructive attempts to escape the plateau.

Most of us have learned to covet the short-term highs we experience at the moment we actually perform a new task well. With discipline, our purpose, and what it takes to achieve it, we begin to be experienced in each step along the way of our life path.

Discipline Includes

PRACTICE

PRACTICE

MORE PRACTICE

... And gives us more freedom

> *If you observe a really happy person, you will find them building a boat, writing a symphony, educating their child, growing double dahlias, or looking for dinosaur eggs in the Gobi Desert. They will not be searching for happiness as if it were a collar button that had rolled under the radiator, striving for it as the goal itself. They will have become aware that they are happy in the course of living life twenty-four crowded hours of each day.*
>
> —W. Beran Wolfe

Five years ago, Carol Ann bought Vance a birthday present of a bronze sculpture of a gymnast. This sculpture is next to the front door of our mountain conference center. As people enter, this is the first thing they see.

The gymnast has to have the discipline to put in hours and years of practice to be able to control his body movements so perfectly while balancing himself on one hand. This mastery was not achieved in some dramatic moment. It came with continual improvement by gradual refinements and small increments that built upon one another.

Everything counts for that gymnast to have the freedom to get all his body parts in exactly the right position that he wants.

The ability of the gymnast to have the freedom to control his body movements comes from the desire to want to practice and practice. He represents to us the gift we give ourselves when we are willing to exercise our own discipline to accomplish what gets us to our

- Purpose;
- Vision;
- Meaningful work;
- Relationships that give us energy;
- Beliefs and behaviors that give peace;
- Reviewing, renewing, and recommitting.

All of these six components of the HHA model are designed to encourage you to think about what is really important in your life. The seventh component, discipline, is what it takes to create structures that aid you in achieving happiness.

Review

- **Happy High Achievers are only 8 percent of high achievers.**

- **Happy High Achievers have a lot of discipline and live their lives first for themselves so that they can give to others in a way that they end up getting more than they give to each relationship.**

In my mind, talent plus knowledge, plus effort account for success.

—Gertrude Samuels

Now let's act! What is one thing you could do consistently well the next 21 days that would make the biggest difference in your life as you further increase your happiness and your high "achievingness"?

As you consider this question, let's revist some of what Csikszentmihalyi has discovered and shared in his book *Flow.*

He finds that people are not at their happiest when they are just having fun or sitting around relaxing. His findings indicate that people report being happiest when they are striving to achieve goals they set for themselves. This kind of happiness is possible even when faced with difficulties. It also does not require resources like money, education, or health.

What is important, according to Csikszentmihalyi, is taking action toward goals and challenges and using your skills fully, doing things that you really want to do. When this occurs, people often are in a state he calls "flow." "Flow" is where you are so involved in achieving what is important to you that you forget yourself.

So, what is so important to you to achieve that you would forget yourself? We believe this is part of what it takes to have discipline. Other important parts are setting goals to achieve your purpose, vision, meaningful work, relationships that give you energy, and beliefs and behaviors that give you peace.

Happy High Achievers' Slogan

If it is to be, it is up to me . . . and you.

Happy High Achievers' Theme Song

Row, row, row your boat

Gently down the stream

Merrily, merrily, merrily, merrily

Life is but a dream

Every person is enthusiastic at times. One person has enthusiasm for thirty minutes, another for thirty days, but it is the person who has it for thirty years who makes a success in life.

—Edward B. Butler

Happy High Achievers have a slogan. It is, "If it is to be, it is up to me . . . and you." These words represent our belief that our lives are up to each of us, and how we define our lives is based on our relationships with you and all the others within our lives.

We have even adopted a Happy High Achiever theme song:

> Row, row, row your boat
>
> Gently down the stream
>
> Merrily, merrily, merrily, merrily
>
> Life is but a dream

We invite you to sing this song, which most of us were taught in kindergarten. Now think about the first line. Does it say to row someone else's boat? Does it say to let someone row your boat? Does it say to let the wind take your boat where it shall? No! It says to "Row, row, row *your* boat!"

Rowing takes both sides of your body to be in balance, getting you to your goal. Out-of-balance rowing looks like going around in circles. Balanced rowing optimizes each stroke toward your castle or your vision coming closer.

"Gently down the stream" is, too, an option in life. We could decide to fight the stream of life. Happy High Achievers don't. They take what's offered and gently leverage it toward their vision in the context of their purpose.

"Merrily, merrily, merrily, merrily" is also a choice. So is grief, grumpiness, and sadness. That's where this song has wisdom in every line. "Life is but a dream" is the fourth reminder. Our wish for you is that your life be your dream and that you're allowing your dream to come true.

Nelson Mandela's Inaugural Speech

Our deepest fear is not that we are inadequate,
Our deepest fear is that we are powerful beyond measure.
It is our light, not our darkness, that most frightens us.
We ask ourselves, who am I to be brilliant, gorgeous,
Talented and fabulous?
Actually, who are you not to be?

You are a child of God.
Your playing small doesn't serve the world.
There is nothing enlightened about shrinking so that
Other people won't feel insecure around you.
We were born to manifest the glory of God within us.

It is not just in some of us; it is in everyone.
And as we let our own light shine, we unconsciously
Give other people permission to do the same.

William Bridges is one of the best-known writers on the subject of transitions. Transitions, he has observed, are generally preceded by a need for changing a part of one's life. For most, the need for change is forced. There is a job loss, a spouse dies, our hometown irrevocably changes. Usually it is a loss.

After a loss, there is then a time of emptiness. It is in this emptiness that we have time and energy to consider what is next in our life choices. In this emptiness, we would do well to consider Nelson Mandela's challenge to rethink our destiny to become the light that we are, acknowledging that which God has loaned us.

In the New Testament, St. Matthew tells us, "Ye are the light of the world. A city that is set on a hill cannot be hid. Neither do men light a candle, and put it under a bushel, but on a candlestick; and it giveth light unto all that are in the house."

Our wish for you is that we may serve as the geese in leading and encouraging you on your flight toward becoming the Happy High Achiever you were born to be. Namaste.

Whether you chose your change or not, there are unlived potentialities within you, interests and talents that you have not yet explored. Transitions clear the ground for new growth. They drop the curtain so the stage can be set for a new scene. What is it, at this point in your life, that is waiting quietly backstage for an entrance cue?

—William Bridges

Resource

Happy High Achiever Progress Report

Rate yourself on each statement, with "1" being the lowest score and "10" being the highest. This assessment will help show the areas with which you feel satisfied and those on which you may wish to work.

1. I am clear about my life mission/purpose/calling. It creates a context or a guiding light with which I live my life each day.

   1   2   3   4   5   6   7   8   9   10

2. I have clarity of vision at multiple milestones in my life. These milestones give me direction and help me make practical decisions much easier, because I am able to choose based on which ones most easily create my vision.

   1   2   3   4   5   6   7   8   9   10

3. There is meaningfulness in my work, so that I am more like the third bricklayer for longer durations. This gives me an "unfair" advantage. I attract resources (clients, staff, and peers), get more done with less effort, and have more satisfaction from my life's work.

   1   2   3   4   5   6   7   8   9   10

4. My relationships energize me. I am consistently aware of the amount of energy I get from each relationship, making adjustments as they serve me best.

   1   2   3   4   5   6   7   8   9   10

5. My beliefs and behaviors create peace in my life, so that I am able to shed chaos and "static" from my life.

   1   2   3   4   5   6   7   8   9   10

6. I am constantly allowing the three R's (review, renewal, and recommitting) to support my staying balanced, much as a juggler is constantly reviewing, renewing, and recommitting to maintain balance.

   1   2   3   4   5   6   7   8   9   10

7. Discipline is an underlying theme that helps me get in the above shape and stay there . . . my system of discipline is working well for me.

   1   2   3   4   5   6   7   8   9   10

Stakeholder Relationship/Trust Scoreboard

Please identify your top five stakeholders and your scores for each.

Stakeholder: One who has power to influence my success (or failure) plus interest in using that power.	Vision: We share the same vision/goals and he or she is supportive of my plan to achieve my vision.	Ethics and a Code of Conduct that align us.	High believability or credibility that my behaviors have earned.	Those I'm perceived to be influenced by ... including coworkers, teachers, friends, and role models ... add to my stakeholder scores.	TOTAL
1.					
2.					
3.					
4.					
5.					

NOTE: Stakeholder scores of 10, 9, or 8 are usually characterized by a flowing relationship involving little written or verbal communications ... as things simply "flow" between the parties. Scores of 7, 6, 5, and 4 usually are characterized as "good" relationships that involve a balance of verbal and written communications to assure alignment. Scores of 3, 2, or 1 usually are characterized by defensiveness, judging, and substantial, defended-type communications.

Bibliography

Bridges, William (1980). *Transitions.* New York: Perseus Books.

Buckingham, Marcus, and Clifton, Donald (2001). *Now, Discover Your Strengths.* New York: The Free Press.

Cashman, Kevin (1999). *Leadership from the Inside Out: Becoming a Leader for Life.* Provo, UT: Executive Excellence Publishing.

Covey, Stephen (1989). *The 7 Habits of Highly Effective People.* New York: Simon & Schuster.

Csikszentmihalyi, Mihaly (1990). *Flow.* New York: Harper & Row.

Davis, Martha, Eshelman, Elizabeth Robbins, & McKay, Matthew (1995). *The Relaxation and Stress Reduction Workbook.* New York: MJF Books.

Epictetus (1994). *The Art of Living.* New York: HarperCollins.

Frankl, Viktor (2000). *Man's Search for Meaning.* Boston: Beacon Press.

Goleman, Daniel (1995). *Emotional Intelligence.* New York: Bantam.

Goleman, Daniel (1998). *Working with Emotional Intelligence.* New York: Bantam Books.

Jones, Laurie Beth (1996). *The Path.* New York: Henry Holt.

Kobasa, Suzanne (1979) *The Hardy Personality* (doctoral dissertation) University of Chicago.

Kouzes, James M., and Posner, Barry Z. (2003). *Leadership Practices Inventory.* San Francisco: Pfeiffer Jossey-Bass.

Leider, Richard J., and Shapiro, David A. (2002). *Repacking Your Bags.* San Francisco: Berrett-Koehler.

Leonard, George (1992). *Mastery.* New York: Plume Books.

O'Neil, John R. (2004). *The Paradox of Success.* New York: Penguin Group.

Peck, Scott (1978). *The Road Less Traveled.* New York: Simon & Schuster.

Ruiz, Don Miguel (1997). *The Four Agreements.* San Rafael, CA: Amber-Allen.

Seligman, Martin (2002). *Authentic Happiness.* New York: Free Press.

**CORWIN
PRESS**

The Corwin Press logo—a raven striding across an open book—represents the union of courage and learning. Corwin Press is committed to improving education for all learners by publishing books and other professional development resources for those serving the field of PreK–12 education. By providing practical, hands-on materials, Corwin Press continues to carry out the promise of its motto: **"Helping Educators Do Their Work Better."**

CPSIA information can be obtained
at www.ICGtesting.com
Printed in the USA
FSOW04n2140291216
29002FS